QUARTER L!FE

Jeremy Stephens

QUARTER L!FE

Crisis Management From History's Greatest 30-Something

Published by Influence Resources
1445 N. Boonville Ave., Springfield, Missouri 65802

Published in association with The Quadrivium Group—Orlando, FL
info@TheQuadriviumGroup.com
and New Vantage Partners—Franklin, TN
info@NewVantagePartners.net

Cover and interior design by Allen Creative—Snellville, GA
Typesetting by Wellspring Design and Jay Victor—Nashville, TN

ISBN: 978-1-936699-13-1

First printing 2012

Printed in United States of America

This book is dedicated to
Abba, my Savior;
Matt, my shepherd;
and Sarah, my sweetheart.

Acknowledgements

Without the tireless efforts of the entire Influence Resources team, the brilliant creativity and editing prowess of Greg and David, the prayers and support of the Grace Midtown community, and the dozens of iced, venti, sugar-free, vanilla Americanos from my local baristas, this book would never have seen the light of day. There are also countless people who have assisted, even in the smallest of ways, to whom I offer my sincerest thanks. But, ultimately, it is the joy God can grant through crisis that has driven this process. Thanks finally go to you, the quarter-lifer, for seeing in yourself the capacity to celebrate, even in trial.

CONTENTS

Before You Read the Introduction

The purpose of *Quarter Life* is to begin a dialogue with fellow "twenty-somethings" encountering the unique challenges facing us when we begin to make steps toward entering the "real world." The study guide questions at the end of each chapter have been written to help the reader engage the material in the book and integrate into his or her own life the lessons and practical steps offered. Because this book is meant to be a starting point, the questions are not intended as homework or merely extraneous. They are provided with the hope that the things God shows you through this process will not fade once the book has been closed. Reading the book and working through the questions won't guarantee that the troubles you are facing will disappear. Rather, they are meant to offer an opportunity for a shift in the thinking that society has ingrained in many of us. Crises are not meant to be avoided. We are taught by Jesus that troubles will come. Any attempt on our part to avoid them will eventually fail. The shift in our thinking occurs when we realize that each trial we face gives us a chance to be further refined, to more fully become the people God wants us to be.

Celebrate your life, troubles and all! My prayer is that through this book you will truly see God has a plan for you. It may not be a plan which looks easy, but it is a plan far better than any you could create for yourself.

In the end, you will see that what you once called a "crisis" has actually brought you closer to God than you ever thought possible.

INTRODUCTION

WHAT IS A QUARTER-LIFE CRISIS?

What is it, in modern, industrialized society, that determines when we officially become adults? Many would argue that it is established by a legal status of some kind—like being old enough to vote, or drink, or buy a handgun. Others might say it follows some achievement, like high school or college graduation, or marriage. Still others might lament that our American culture has lost all indicators for when one truly becomes an adult, and the concept is more relative, changing from person to person.

If I were to think back over my life thus far and attempt to pinpoint my transition from adolescence to adulthood, I would say …

… I'm still in transition.

The path of my life has just navigated its trickiest route – a winding, convoluted tangle of roads, traversing a multitude of emotional and spiritual terrains. Looking back, I would call it a learning experience. But in the midst of it, a much better word would be "crisis."

I track most of my personal history by the churches I have attended. Depending on what age you ask about, I can probably reference what pastor I had at the time or what church project I was working on. At about age five, it would be Dr. Ron Long and the kids' musical: "Oh Me, Oh My, Oh Nehemiah!" About age sixteen, it would be Pastor Mark Paul and serving on the Youth Group Council. Ask me about age eighteen, and it would be Pastor Louie Giglio and preparing to enter the ministry.

Ever since I can remember, my memories are painted with the colors of stained glass windows and the tastes of grape juice and communion wafers. My parents raised me in a firmly Southern Baptist environment, and all signs upon my exiting high school pointed towards my becoming a pastor in an equally-firm Southern Baptist church. I graduated high school, packed my belongings, and headed off to Bible college.

Twelve months passed. I quit Bible college (because of a lack of interest), entered a community college (because of a lack of purpose), and moved back in with my parents (because of a lack of funds).

This began my downward spiral toward crisis.

I eventually finished my undergrad degree at a state school. With that bachelor's degree in psychology, I immediately landed a job at a coffee shop. That job transitioned into a job at a chiropractic office, which transitioned into a job teaching kindergarten, where I currently spend my daytime hours. In the midst of all this, I worked at a summer camp where God blessed my soul by allowing me to meet the woman I would marry.

I understand that nothing in that story shouts the word "crisis."

Allow me to continue.

Fast forward to my third year of teaching kindergarten. I am more-than-happily married, we have two dogs, I have an amazing job, and …it's Christmastime.

Christmastime to me is the truest picture of heaven on earth. Had you visited our apartment at any point from November 15th to January 20th you would have been greeted by a porch so brightly illuminated that even the Griswolds would be jealous. I am the guy who drives to work in October with his windows down, blasting Bing Crosby.

However this year, it is three days before Christmas, and I am drowning in depression. Dark thoughts attack my waking hours. These thoughts are made even scarier because I have never before experienced depression. My life up to that point had been a happy-go-lucky one, and apart from a few typical stresses, I had my feet firmly planted on the field of optimism. My dark thoughts went like this:

"This will all end one day. I'm getting older and older, and I can't stop it. One day I'll look back and see that my life has flown by, and it's over, and there is no way to get that life back.

"I like my job now, but it isn't where I want to be forever. Did I waste my money on that degree? Do I really want to spend forty years wiping six-year-olds' noses?

"We live in an apartment, and I'm almost thirty. We barely have enough money in the bank for groceries. Could I call one of my parents for help? I can't do that …

"What do I really believe? Is there actually something out there bigger than me, bigger than the universe?"

At first, I had no idea why these thoughts were popping into my head. But I couldn't live like this. I tried everything to make myself feel better: playing video games, getting my friends' opinions, distracting myself with parties and get-togethers, etc., etc.

I searched online to figure out what was going on with me. That's when I found out that the problem is all too common. I began to call it a crisis and came to find it was far more widespread than I thought. Everywhere I looked, I found people my age confronting the same thoughts and feelings. I found references to it in blogs, articles about it in research journals, descriptions and guidance groups for it in my community. But I also discovered that finding a solution to the problem was much harder. Sure, there are blogs dedicated to the subject, but most of them consisted of telling people to tough it out or get therapy. The rest pointed to self-help books, exercise plans, and anti-depressants.

What I needed is Who I had needed for a long time, but He wasn't in any of the places I looked. You may have noticed that, after childhood, I didn't mention God by name very much. That wasn't an accident.

That was because God and I didn't spend a lot of time together after I graduated from high school. It wasn't His choosing – it was mine. The so-called Christians around me were phonies. The people who took on Christ's name were acting much less Christ-like than most atheists I knew.

Looking back, though, showed me that I was a phony, too. I disregarded a Father who had loved me my whole life, just because of a few people in the church, all of whom (including myself) are wholly imperfect and undeserving of His love. As a result, I acted in a way I didn't like. I abandoned an education that would have offered me a fountain of godly knowledge for one which showed me how the world works when Jesus isn't the focus.

It was all in His name – or so I thought. I was seeking what I felt God *should* be. "If He is the Truth," I thought, "I can find Him wherever I look." I had failed to realize that, without faith, the truth can be a tricky thing to determine. Without the ultimate Creator of truth, how can we hope to discover the truth He created?

Perhaps our culture of relativism led to my crisis. Perhaps I was confused because there were so many apparently viable options. Maybe I simply needed to find the truth within myself. I adopted a type of *Star Wars* credo, feeling the force of the god within – but the crisis continued.

Perhaps I needed to exercise more. After all, we are a much smarter generation than the ones who wrote the "sacred" texts. We understand more about how the brain works and have determined that running can act as an anti-depressant. But even after exercising, I was still in a crisis, only sweating.

Not until later, I grabbed the little-used and dusty Bible that remained in my gigantic library of postmodern ramblings. I couldn't put it down. I was reading the same verses from my childhood but for the very first time.

God reached down and picked me up out of the dirt. He was there all along, letting me roam, letting me find my way, because He loved me enough—just as He loves you enough—to never violate my free will. He was waiting for the moment I needed Him most to remind me He has known and cared for me all along.

There is a term for people in their twenties and thirties who face struggles like the ones through which I have recently trudged. It is a newly-branded term, with most sources claiming its first usage in the book *Quarterlife Crisis: The Unique Challenges of Life in Your Twenties*, co-authored by Abby Wilner and Alexandra Robbins. Though behaviors and attitudes associated with this period of life were first identified by Erik H. Erikson, its manifestation in modern society holds characteristics that are more in line with Erikson's adolescence stage. As a people group, we are maturing much more slowly than on Erikson's timeline.

A Quarter-Life Crisis (QLC*), generally speaking, is that period of life faced (typically by those in modern Western society) between the early twenties and early thirties.

The specific issues that arise include:

- The struggle of confronting one's mortality (especially as our parents begin to age), wondering how our own lives will end and preparing for death's inevitability;
- Developing autonomous beliefs and opinions, retreating from the comfortable shelter of our parents' views on politics and religion;
- Being nostalgic for the simpler times of high school and college, free from the pressures of mortgages, career paths, and income-tax returns;
- Struggling with financial independence, budgeting our paltry earnings towards groceries and car payments;

* I use the acronym *QLC* interchangeably with the phrase "quarter-life crisis" not simply because it is easier to type, but because acronyms seem less intimidating.

- Creating and maintaining friendships and relationships, looking forward to marriage and family life;
- Pursuing the beginnings of a career, as we are daunted by the prospect of choosing one job, possibly for the rest of our lives.

At first glance, you may sense similarities in both name and attributes to the more commonly-spoken about mid-life crisis that plagues many people as they enter their forties. But the QLC is a far cry from the drastic haircut or sports car purchase often associated with the mid-life crisis. Whereas a mid-life crisis is a time that many spend reflecting on their twenties and thirties, longing for what could have been or should have been, a quarter-life crisis comes as a response to *not even having an idea* of what should come next. A mid-life crisis asks "What if?" while a quarter-life crisis asks "What now?" To many, the twenties and thirties crisis is the defining step of their whole life. As we approach it, (whether or not we know what to call it), we can see that the things dealt with during this period of time are those things which will determine the direction our lives will go for the rest of our time on the planet.

While the creation of a family, career, and financial stability are all occurring simultaneously, one must add spiritual worries to the mix as well. Not only must I search out a companion, a job, and a way to pay my bills, but I must balance these things alongside the deeper issues of where my life is headed.

It's no coincidence that Jesus lived to be in His thirties. As our spiritual and moral frame of reference for how to live, Jesus represents the only perfect human and the only person to emerge successfully from all temptations, thoughts, and life situations that humans face – without giving in to a sinful nature. His responses and guidance offer us signposts to navigate through struggle in the way God would have us do it – with our morals and integrity intact. The major milestones setting up our lives occur *prior* to the age at which Jesus gave His life for us on the cross. He experienced struggles with mortality, autonomy, career, relationships, and finance. He went through those things so we can have a Guide on our own journeys. He ultimately gave His life so we can have hope in *all* the journeys of our life.

I do not assume that the quarter-life crisis is a worldwide phenomenon. This book makes the assumption that it is prevalent mainly in American society. Yes, there are phenomena in other cultures that can result in similar stresses (take, for instance, the topics of hikikomori and parasite singles in Japan). However, American culture cultivates a unique blend of materialism, narcissism, and individuality that provides the perfect melting pot for someone in their twenties or thirties to face this struggle. Also, because of American consumerism and technology, we have a much denser, much more vocal, quarter-life population.

The struggles many people our age are facing exist because there are no significant rites of passage in America anymore. Prior to this generation, the American ideal of a nuclear family and post-depression career were our rites of passage. One need only look at *Leave It to Beaver* or *The Waltons* to get a glimpse of the goals that past generations of American young people were pursuing as they reached their twenties. In societies with clearly-defined *rites* of passage there are also clearly-defined *routes* of passage. With a set marker for where one should be by a certain age, it becomes much simpler to focus one's energies on a specific task or tasks. It would have been much easier for me to navigate this winding road if there had been a map in my hand or signposts along the way.

A quarter-life crisis can take many forms. Though there has been a response to the issue, a few minutes searching the Internet will reveal that there has not been much in the way of telling how a *Christian* can best respond – or rather how God can direct us to respond. This book is an attempt to encourage a God-centered discussion of this unique period in life.

Again, I feel as if I'm still transitioning into adulthood. Although I'm much closer than I have ever been, maybe becoming an adult is realizing that we will always have some growing up to do.

Much of this book draws on my own experience. So, each chapter of the book begins with a section called "Introspection," in which I describe my own feelings and dealings with the subject matter. Each chapter then moves into an "Interview" section, where someone more educated on the specific topic (pastor, author, musician, or entrepreneur) offers his or her perspective. Finally, each chapter concludes with a section called "Inspiration." This offers the unique and eternally-wise perspective we can find in the life and teachings of Jesus Christ. Although I recommend reading the book start to finish, you might want to skip ahead and read the "Inspiration" sections first. After all, why listen to the warm-up band when you can get into the real deal for free?

In this book, I don't position myself as a great disseminator of truths, passing down my lofty knowledge from pulpit or soapbox. From my perspective, you and I are just beggars in a world impoverished of truth – and

I want to tell you where I've found a morsel of bread to help fill the longing.

There is Truth to be found, and He loves you.

Engage

Discussion

The questions here and following each chapter can be answered either on your own or within a group. If you are completing this guide by yourself, prayerfully consider going through it with another person or small group. The topics engaged in this book are meant to be an opportunity for group discussions because of the encouragement of shared experience.

Talk with your group or partner about how the following statements make you feel when you hear them. Are they something you hear a lot? Do you identify with the things being said? How do these statements fit within the framework of Christianity?

1. You will feel fulfilled as soon as you find the right career.
2. Having a family will make you happy.
3. You make your own outcome. It is up to you to find success.
4. Religion is good for morals but is too outdated to apply practically.
5. Just hang in there, and you will survive any trials you are going through.

Reflection

Based on reading the Introduction, do you feel like you better understand why the transition out of college can be such a difficult one? Many people would readily admit to wrestling with some of the issues we will discuss in the book. Some might be surprised to find that these trials are so common among twenty-somethings. Prior to picking up this book, had you ever heard of a quarter-life crisis?

Reflect on the following questions as you prepare to read the first chapter.

1. Looking back at your own life, how much would you say the person you are now is made up of your family's religious practices?

2. Have you ever sought out answers for the struggles you face? If you have, where did you look? If you haven't, why not?
3. Do you think that, right now, you find your identity more in your beliefs or your trials?
4. Has society's view of adulthood and success made you more or less confident? How much of your definition of success is shaped by society?
5. What would you say are the biggest hurdles confronting you right now? If you find yourself in a quarter-life crisis, how are those hurdles compounded for you?

Activity
Write down the top five things you would label as trials right now. Compare them with someone else, and see how many are the same. Save the list for when you finish reading the book.

Before You Read Chapter 1

There is one issue in this book every single person who is currently alive will one day have to face. Death. How difficult is the topic of mortality for you to contemplate? Many of us grew up with a view of mortality which said it is best to avoid discussing it altogether. But is this really a healthy way to deal with the most common of human experiences?

As you read Chapter 1, think about your own experience with death. Is your view on it one that allows for the greatness of God to be shown? After all, if we don't admit its terror, we undermine the power of God in conquering it.

CHAPTER 1

DEATH AND PANCAKES—MORTALITY AND THE QLC

"For while we are still in this tent, we groan, being burdened—not that we would be unclothed, but that we would be further clothed, so that what is mortal may be swallowed up by life."
2 Corinthians 5:4

Introspection

Confronting one's own mortality is perhaps one of the most common, and most debilitating, aspects of the QLC. I address this topic first for somewhat selfish reasons. It was the most difficult part of getting through my own QLC. Death is the biggest challenge we as humans face, the most unique, mind-bending concept we can fathom. In all its uniqueness, death holds a firm grasp on us because it is one of a small number of experiences that is common to absolutely everyone. If we can confront the idea of our mortality, we will have much more hope in handling the other important issues in our lives.

The uncertainty of a person's future, paired with the view that our parents are aging (that is, nearing their own final exit), often leads us to become more aware of our inevitable departure from this current state. Through childhood and adolescence, it can seem that our parents do not really age and that the life we know will always remain the way it has been. However, as we reach our twenties, reality begins to set in. For me, this reality crashed down on me in the days leading up to Christmas one year. As I mentioned, Christmas is my favorite holiday. You can safely assume I have been referred to as one of Santa's elves on more than one occasion, thanks to my obsession with decorating. There is no other time of the year in which I can be found happier or more in the moment. However, for reasons of which I was not fully aware at the time, this particular Christmas season was characterized only by sadness.

I remember heading out with my wife for a pancake breakfast at our favorite restaurant – only to return hours later in the pits of despair because we dined next to a table full of white-haired senior citizens. One of my favorite things to do had been ruined with the inescapable portrayal of human mortality right in front of my face. It didn't matter that these old folks were having a better time than anyone else in the restaurant. What I saw was a picture of where my life was headed ... *The End.* I had little control over these feelings because my QLC had come as a random, quick, powerful, and wholly unexpected event.

Yes, there are legitimate concerns surrounding the idea of death. There are going to be situations in which thoughts of death are unavoidable. Sometimes they can even be healthy ways to value the time God gives us. The prospect of terminal illness will require a certain level of constant awareness of mortality. Losing someone close to you can stir up thoughts about what happens after this life.

However, if healthy young people, without prompting, are constantly preoccupied with mortality, they should take the time to evaluate how they have become so absorbed in the topic – and how best to address their concerns.

When it happened to me, I was not sick. I had not recently lost anyone close to me. I was simply in the throes of my personal quarter-life crisis. Looking back now, I know this was God's way of showing me He is in control – and that ultimately there is nothing to fear about our passing.

But getting to that point took some work.

Our culture, as a whole, attempts to remove the concept of death from everyday dialogue as much as possible. In our pursuit of youth and immortality—through plastic surgeries, wonder drugs, embryonic stem cell research, and the like—we have become ignorant of the psychological and spiritual significance that facing our mortality can hold. Can you remember the last time you saw a new church built alongside a cemetery, or a sermon on God's providence in regard to death and dying? If you were to close your eyes and think about celebrities over the age of 50, wouldn't it be easier to identify those who have *not* had plastic surgery to look younger?

It is this denial of death that has led many thanatologists (researchers on death) to conclude that we have lost the ability to analyze our mortality. Dr. Elizabeth Kubler-Ross, in her seminal work *On Death and Dying*, says that "In a society where death is regarded as a taboo, discussion of it is regarded as morbid, and children are excluded with the presumption and pretext that it would be 'too much' for them."[1] How, then, can we ever hope to overcome these feelings of imminence and looming mortality so common to those enduring a quarter-life crisis?

A good place to start is to examine how other cultures have handled death. All cultures throughout human history have developed a belief in some sort of afterlife. The ancient Egyptians are thought to have had one of the earliest systematized views on life after death. The Egyptians offered a complicated story that includes a feather of truth and justice, a goddess' headdress, even a soul-eating demon. As complex as that story became, it is interesting to see how the Egyptians placed an even larger emphasis on *preparing* for the afterlife than on *enjoying* the present life. They viewed what happens in the hereafter as exponentially more important than anything that could possibly happen now.

Another culture with a complex view of the afterlife were the Zoroastrians. They believed that following death, the spirit of the person remained at the dead body's head, singing for three days before departing for the Kingdom of the Dead. Greek and Nordic traditions described a three-tiered system in the afterlife, with the highest level of afterlife existence reserved for those who have died heroically, the middle level for those neither heroic nor immoral, and the lower level for those who have been quite naughty.

Hindus, as well as quite a few Orthodox Jews from the East, believe in a system of reincarnation, which promises that whatever a person does during life on earth, either good or bad, is used to determine what form one will take upon the start of their next life. Jewish people of the Old Testament period and many Christians today believe that upon death, all souls enter a place known as Sheol. There they wait, either in paradise or torment, for a time of final judgment, where the righteous and unrighteous are separated, and then sent to their eternal destinations.

In tracing biblical history back to Adam (the man whom the Bible identifies as the first human being), Christians conclude that death was not the original intent for God's creation of humanity. Prior to that pesky incident with the fruit, the snake, and shameful nudity, humans were all set to enjoy an immortal existence in a garden with the Creator. (If you don't know the story, open a Bible to the first page and start reading). Amazingly, God wanted us to *choose* Him rather than follow Him like robots, so He gave us free will. We will talk more about this in the chapter on autonomy. But for now, to say the least, this freedom was first abused in the Garden of Eden, and human beings have been dying ever since.

Against the backdrop of mortality, though, we must remember that humans have been made in the image of God. As such, while we intuit that death is something unnatural and foreign, we also are inclined to view our bodily death as not being the final end.

Admittedly, this list of belief systems is short and far from complete. My purpose is to show that the discussion about "what happens when we die" has been going on since the first bucket was kicked. A culture's view of the afterlife is the primary factor in how its people view death. (For instance, ancient Egyptians believed that we each have three souls and that our bodies must survive the transition of death intact in order for those three souls to function properly. This explains why there was so much emphasis on the Egyptian tradition of embalming.)

The word *death* or one of its variants is used more than 370 times in the Bible. Not all of these instances refer to a physical, bodily death, which is a separation of a person's body and soul. The Bible often speaks of a spiritual death, which is the separation of a human from God. Each time, however, death is seen as a separation of two things. Those who consider the Bible to be sacred see sin as the original cause of death and therefore see death as an unnatural part of our existence. Death is often faced harshly in the Bible. ("Then Jacob tore his garments, and put sackcloth on his loins, and mourned for his son many days. All his sons and all his daughters sought to comfort him; but he refused to be comforted, and said, 'No, I shall go down to Sheol to my son, mourning.' Thus his father bewailed him." (Genesis 37:34-35) But sometimes, when a righteous person dies in Scripture, death is seen as a time of rejoicing because they have returned to be with God ("Abraham breathed his last and died in a good old age, an old man and full of years, and was gathered to his people." (Genesis 25:8)

While in the midst of my QLC, I often worried about the inevitability of death. I avoided scary movies, threw away my Goth music, only played video games meant for children – basically avoiding the topic altogether. Unfortunately, in practice, trying to dodge our mortality serves only to remove ourselves from the necessary discussion. Just as our society cannot hope to tackle the subject and learn from death if we avoid it altogether, we as individuals – and as Christians – only hurt ourselves by sidestepping it. We must face death head on. Not until I stared mortality right in the face could I see through it and find God waiting on the other side. He does not want us to worry constantly about it – but He also does not want us to ignore it either. Yes, death is inevitable. Until Christ's return to earth, all people on this planet will someday wind up in a casket. However, there is joy to be found in that realization.

I mentioned earlier that the Bible tells us death is unnatural and entered into our world only because of an abuse of our divinely-given free will. But by that same free will, death can be removed from our world. While we still face the unknowns associated with physical death, it can be seen as a bridge back to where we were meant to be ... in the presence of our Creator. I hope for you that, if you are facing those difficult thoughts on death and dying, you can see there is a way in which we can rejoice in death and take the sting out of its inevitability.

Interview

In putting together the "Interview" sections of this book, I prayerfully considered who best to approach about each topic, making sure that his or her profession complemented and encompassed all the aspects of the topic to offer you a thorough investigation. Where, then, should I turn about the topic of mortality? A mortician, perhaps? A coroner? Possibly, but those folks interact with people who are, well, dead. Those who are already-passed are not likely to be reading this book. No, I needed to speak with someone who deals hands-on with mortality issues but also helps those left behind in their grief. I also needed someone the right age so he or she could identify with the specific challenges mortality presents to those at quarter-life.

I needed to speak with my pastor.

Matt Reynolds became the senior pastor of our church about two years ago when we had about twenty members. Since then, God has blessed us with over a thousand members, mostly college students. The Spirit has been leading Matt, at just 27-years-old, to guide this young flock in outreach among the downtrodden in the one of the largest U.S. cities: Atlanta, Georgia.

Pastors are uniquely qualified to talk about mortality. They typically attend more funerals in a year than most people do in a lifetime. Matt is no exception. I approached him about the topic of mortality and how it affects people in quarter-life crisis.

My first question: Why is the quarter-life part of growing up so closely tied to thinking about one's death, since it is still such a young age?

I think people at this age start to consider that their life is going to end one day, because up to that point your life has been mapped out for you. You know what you're supposed to do and what the norms are. You go to high school and get good grades. You go to college and get a good education. You get a good job …but in that transition period after getting a degree, especially now with the economy like it is, there's this sense that says: "I've been becoming this specific person, but who am I really?" There are a lot of identity questions … "What do I want to be known for, and live for?" Your body starts to change; your mindset changes. You realize you're getting older, and there is a sense of depression about starting at the bottom of some totem pole somewhere just to survive and make it. There is almost a death there already, a pressure to become a new person you know nothing about. You've invested in this degree and this education for so long, and now there is no coaching—no advice given—on what to do next. People start to think about this new reality and have to die to the person they have been so used to being.

Next question: As a pastor, what did you feel the role of believers should be in a society that often ignores the idea of death altogether?

The role of believers in society is to give people a biblical perspective on death and mortality. Jesus says in Luke, "What good is it for man to gain the whole world and lose his soul?" And this is talking about really having a fear of the Lord as our Judge … who will decide your destiny in one way or the other. We have the responsibility and privilege to show people that truth. There is so much more for which we are made … we are created for an eternal destiny, and we can decide what kind of eternal destiny we have. Believers have the unique task of talking about that choice.

Question #3: Do believers, then, have more responsibility in how they present themselves to the world?

Jesus says we can look at the world as if we are foreigners in it, or as if it is a place in which we spend our lives chasing and striving after things like the American dream (which is a lie anyway), trying to fill our lives with things that will fade away.

> *As believers, we can be free from the things of the world … from empty achievements we accomplish by living to satisfy another master. Do we follow what the world gives, or do we leave those things and follow Christ? We can live in the world while still following Jesus and have lives full of significance and purpose. That way, whether our lives end at age 27, 57, or 97, we can present those things to the Lord as riches and show Him how we have been good stewards with what He has given us. We need to set our minds on things above, and all these things … even the things on earth … will be added unto us.*

I wondered out loud: "Even Christians struggle with death sometimes. What is the best thing a believer can do to redirect those negative thoughts?"

> *Find your joy and satisfaction in the Lord, because when that relationship is the top priority, you are free. There is a sense of peace, perspective and revelation that God has come. When you turn to Him and ask His opinion on things, request His wisdom. That will open up a whole new world to you. In Ecclesiastes, when Solomon talks about how "there is nothing new under the sun"…a statement that reflects the stress and confusion of living apart from God …they think,* "We're going to die like everyone else, so what is the point?" *Leaving it at that is a lie. When we live in the light of God's truth, everything is new under the sun. God has an eternal purpose for each of us, and when we seek that, everything becomes new. Your job, your family, the journey becomes new. Tomorrow has never existed before …this will be a new day when God can give us the peace and confidence to live in that new experience … and it is unlike any other experience in the world.*

Inspiration

QLC sufferers have an ally in their battle to come to grips with the inevitability of death: history's greatest thirty-something. The inevitability of Jesus' own death was paraded in front of Him, even while He was still an infant in the manger.

The Gospel of Matthew chronicles the arrival of a group of Magi, or wise men, who had come to celebrate the birth of Jesus. They were deeply changed when they met Jesus. God spoke to them in a dream following their visit, telling them to avoid Herod, even though the Hebrew king had been the one who first directed them to the Christ. The Magi were even kind enough to bring gifts to the Christ-child. They presented gold, frankincense, and myrrh. It is easy to understand why gold was in their gift bag. I have often wished that this tradition could have continued through the time of my own birth. Although the reason for the other two gifts is less obvious, upon closer examination, a curious foreshadowing is found. Frankincense and myrrh were both used during funerals – frankincense for incense and myrrh as an embalming aid. Myrrh was also mixed with alcohol to numb criminals' pain prior to their deaths. Such a drink was offered to Jesus as He endured His day of suffering. Mark 15:22-23 says: "Then they brought Jesus to the place called Golgotha (which means the place of a skull). And they offered him wine mixed with myrrh; but he did not take it." If death was always so present a thought in Jesus' mind, how does He address the concept of death?

1. Jesus' views on death shaped His views on life.

Though it is the central idea of the Christian faith – that Jesus died to be our Redeemer – the topic of death is one that Jesus speaks surprisingly little about. When He does, it is often used to *enhance* how we live. As Jesus walked along a road one day, two men approached Him, offering to follow Him in His travels. Luke 9:57-60 tells us the story:

> As they were going along the road, someone said to him, "I will follow you wherever you go." And Jesus said to him, "Foxes have holes, and birds of the air have nests; but the Son of Man has nowhere to lay his head." To another He said, "Follow me." But he said, "Lord, first let me go and bury my father." But Jesus said to him, "Let the dead bury their own dead; but as for you, go and proclaim the kingdom of God."

It is obvious from this passage that, as Christians, we are called to a life of passionate dedication to the cause God has given us. Death is inevitable, yes. But it should not be our focus.

This is not to say Jesus understated the emotional turmoil that comes from losing someone close to us. Upon hearing that His good friend had gotten sick and died, and seeing the pain it was causing his close friends, the Scriptures offer their shortest, but perhaps most touching, account of Jesus' humanity. John 11:35 says: "Jesus wept."

Death was all around Jesus – from His walks through the towns, healing those close to death, raising the dead, to His final meal with those closest to Him. Prior to being arrested in the garden, Jesus spent an evening with His disciples, offering the most intimate portrayal of what death meant to Him. Rather than avoid the topic of death, He shared a meal with His closest friends and talked plainly about what was about to happen to Him. Death, originally caused by sin, would now be conquered through His death.

2. Jesus' views on life shaped His views on the afterlife.

Throughout what would be considered His prime quarter-life crisis period, ages 30 to 33, Jesus accomplished an entire career's worth of evangelical ministry. He healed. He fed. He preached. He guided. He loved. It was not the people who knew the most about history or philosophy or religion who accepted Jesus and His message. In fact, the knowledge experts during Jesus' time, the Pharisees, were the very ones He often condemned for their ignorance. His message of redemption was not presented esoterically. It was not offered in an apologetics classroom. It was given in parables, stories taken directly from everyday life. People were struggling through the same serious issues we face today: poverty, disease, human trafficking. They did not need someone to tell them death was inevitable. They already knew that and saw it all around them. They needed someone to guide them, to give them what their hearts were longing for: the hope for redemption and fellowship with God. This desire, often buried under the iniquity of our humanness, stubbornly remains with us since we are created in the image of God.

Jesus offered redemption – eternal life – through an open invitation to all who would seek it. Although His stories were simple, they were not for the hard-hearted. A sincere desire for the love of God was required to understand them. In their simplicity resided a deep understanding of what is to come after death – and why not to fear it.

Matthew 13:44-46 presents two examples of this:

> The kingdom of heaven is like treasure hidden in a field, which someone found and hid; then in his joy he goes and sells all that he has and buys that field. Again, the kingdom of

> heaven is like a merchant in search of fine pearls; on finding one pearl of great value, he went and sold all that he had and bought it.

Jesus is telling His listeners that, though costly, the Kingdom of Heaven is available to all who seek it and that it is worth more than any other thing they could ever hope to obtain.

The greatest testament to Christ's focus on the afterlife – on its importance and His triumph over death – can be found in the story of the rich man and Lazarus:

> There was a rich man who was dressed in purple and fine linen and who feasted sumptuously every day. And at his gate lay a poor man named Lazarus, covered with sores, who longed to satisfy his hunger with what fell from the rich man's table; even the dogs would come and lick his sores. The poor man died and was carried away by the angels to be with Abraham. The rich man also died and was buried. In Hades, where he was being tormented, he looked up and saw Abraham far away with Lazarus by his side. (Luke 16:19-23)

This story would have been striking to those who hung out with Jesus. They knew well how difficult a life of sickness and poverty could be, how often death seemed a welcome alternative. But in speaking about death, and ultimately flipping it on its head, Jesus uses this story to show that wealth or status is not the pathway to eternal life with God. Anyone, no matter what their place in society, could be redeemed.

Jesus goes on to offer a striking observation of how a hardened heart cannot hope to experience God's redemption, even when presented with an actual resurrection. Even today this holds true. We have been presented with an undeniable resurrection – the raising of Jesus Christ from the dead – and still, people continue to live for this life only.

3. Jesus' views on the afterlife shaped His views on God.

As people in a world of instant gratification and overstimulation, it can be easy to lose our focus on things of true importance. Perhaps that is our modern curse. We have simply gotten too busy to think about death, and when we do it is devastating. But Jesus knew the purpose of our existence here on earth is not to do all we can to live as long as possible. It is not to eat healthy, exercise, take our vitamins, or use anti-aging cream. It is not to stay young, to look young, or to feel young. It is, rather, to love. Love, according to Jesus, is the reason for which we have been created. Love shapes how we interact with our world, because it shapes how God interacts with us. We are not, on our own, worthy of the life or the afterlife that God would have for us. We must accept His mercy and reclaim His grace. These offer our only hope of spending an eternity with Him.

One of Jesus' most eye-opening visions of what the afterlife will be like comes in His response to some Sadducees who had tried to back Him into a corner with a question about marriage and heaven. Mark 12:18-27 recounts the exchange:

> Some Sadducees, who say there is no resurrection, came to him and asked him a question, saying, "Teacher, Moses wrote for us that 'if a man's brother dies, leaving a wife but no child, the man shall marry the widow and raise up children for his brother.' There were seven brothers; the first married and, when he died, left no children; and the second married her and died, leaving no children; and the third likewise; none of the seven left children. Last of all, the woman herself died. In the resurrection whose wife will she be? For the seven had married her." Jesus said to them, "Is not this the reason you are wrong, that you know neither the scriptures nor the power of God? For when they rise from the dead, they neither marry nor are given in marriage, but are like angels in heaven. And as for the dead being raised, have you not read in the book of Moses, in the story about the bush, how God said to him, 'I am the God of Abraham, the God of Isaac, and the God of Jacob'? He is God not of the dead, but of the living; you are quite wrong."

Jesus was often at the receiving end of some wily verbal assaults. Every time, however, He outwitted his assailants by offering them a simple truth. Life is important, and it is important to live it for God. Marriage is important and is something that should be cherished during this life. The Sadducees denied the existence of an afterlife, which became one of their main points of conflict with the Pharisees. They were attempting to disprove the existence of the afterlife with a logical conundrum. With a sweep of perfect thinking, Jesus – holder of all knowledge regarding what is to come – showed them with crystal clarity that our earthly rules do not apply after this life is over. Marriage, though offered by God as a comfort to us during our physical lives, does not continue following our deaths. Neither do our current, natural bodies. Moses, Abraham, Isaac, and Jacob all lived physical lives and died physical deaths, but to God's glory, they are not dead. God is the God of the living, having given them glorified bodies—sinless as Jesus was sinless and fit to be in His presence.

Jesus viewed God as His Father, the Giver of life, the Holder of eternity, and the Path to perfection. He taught of an everlasting life found in God to those who seek Him and an everlasting torment to those who deny Him. Jesus saw that our physical lives are precious and important. He came with healing, compassion, and tolerance. He also saw our spiritual lives as even more precious, even more important. That is why He didn't teach a life of healthy eating and safety but of devotion, no matter the cost, to Him.

The Father sent the Son to be His Word, to enlighten the world, and to redeem us through His death so we can live our lives emulating His own. Death is not to be feared for those who believe and live for Him. Death is to be acknowledged as unavoidable because it is simply a deadline by which we must spread His truth to others. John 12:49-50 tells us:

> For I have not spoken on my own, but the Father who sent me has himself given me a commandment about what to say and what to speak. And I know that his commandment is eternal life. What I speak, therefore, I speak just as the Father has told me.

4. Jesus' views on God shaped His views on death.

Although Jesus has shown that death need not be feared, it can still be terrifying because it is such an unknown experience. No one can know what to expect because it only happens once to any given person. Jesus knew throughout His life that He was destined to be our atoning sacrifice. Although we know little about his childhood and teenage years, as soon as He begins His ministry as an adult, He speaks of His impending death. The Bible tells us in Mark that He devoted personal time to telling His disciples that He was on a path leading toward death – but they didn't understand. Mark 9:31-34 says:

> For he was teaching his disciples, saying to them, "The Son of Man is to be betrayed into human hands, and they will kill him, and three days after being killed, he will rise again." But they did not understand what he was saying and were afraid to ask him.

Jesus' message was clear, but not until He had died did the impact of His death sink in to those around Jesus. Even the night He was to be arrested, Jesus went with His closest friends to the garden to pray. He tried three times to get His friends to sit up with Him. And three times His friends simply fell asleep. The only person He could truly talk to about it was God, His Father. Matthew 26:36-44 describes the scene:

> Then Jesus went with them to a place called Gethsemane; and he said to his disciples, "Sit here while I go over there and pray." He took with him Peter and the two sons of Zebedee, and began to be grieved and agitated. Then he said to them, "I am deeply grieved, even to death; remain here, and stay awake with me." And going a little farther, he threw himself on the ground and prayed, "My Father, if it is possible, let this cup pass from me; yet not what I want but what you want." Then he came to the disciples and found them sleeping; and he said to Peter, "So, could you not stay awake with me one hour? Stay awake and pray that you may not come into the time of trial; the spirit indeed is willing, but the flesh is weak." Again he went away for the second time and prayed, "My Father, if this cannot pass unless I drink it, your will be done." Again he came and found them sleeping, for their eyes were heavy. So leaving them again, he went away and prayed for the third time, saying the same words.

In our times of sadness, we reach out to those around us. We try to explain to friends or family members how we are feeling. They might sympathize, but they often cannot fully empathize. Jesus knew the only One who would always be able to understand our suffering is God. Each time Jesus prayed in the garden that night, He acknowledged that death was not something He desired but something He feared. He then takes it a step farther than many of us may be willing to do. Each time, He ended His prayer admitting that we are not the ones in control of our destinies, that we are not the ones who get to decide how long our lives should be. The One Who holds our existence in His hands is the same One Who created us. God the Father grants us life. God the Father grants us all our happiness, all our joys, and every single breath. God the Father suffers when we suffer. God the Father did not want death as a part of our experience. Through our humanity, sin entered the world, and death followed. But while its sting is temporary, our life with God can be everlasting.

From a human perspective, it is rational and natural to fear death. Fearing death is appropriate because death is an unnatural thing. We were not created to die. However, though our physical bodies have been tainted with the impurity of sin, Jesus has conquered death in order to redeem us back into the eternal favor we were meant to have with our Heavenly Father. The QLC, for many of us, is the first time we really consider our inevitable end. For some, it is a welcome reassurance of the salvation we have in Christ. For others, it may be just the impetus needed to open our hearts to the God who is always waiting for us to return to Him.

Having sorted through so much about my own mortality, I realize that I didn't have to despair after an otherwise-pleasant pancake breakfast with my wife. In some of the most difficult times I encountered during my QLC, I could see people like the ones in the restaurant only in terms of their age – and for the window into my own future that they provided. As a believer, though, I can see them as a reflection of the joy we have in our lives by simply accepting that the closer we get to the inevitable moment so often feared and dreaded, the closer we are getting to the glorious reunion we can have with our Savior. The more we realize we were not originally intended to experience death, the more we can fall in love with the Savior for His sacrifice and promise that death does not end it all.

Engage

Discussion

Before meeting with your group or partner, review the following questions. Write down your answers as well. When you meet, be ready to share your answers and listen to others.

1. When you think about your own mortality, are your first thoughts more related to how Christianity faces death or how society deals with it?

2. How has death within your family or circle of friends affected your faith? Do you feel that now, in your quarter-life stage, you are more or less spiritually prepared to handle it?
3. Do you see death as something to avoid discussing or something inevitable that should be talked about? Explain.
4. How does the experience of Jesus in His final days shape your view of mortality?
5. What are some ways that your view of mortality has changed after reading this chapter?

Reflection

This chapter opens the book because of the topic's enormous impact on human experience. Death has been discussed, debated, and defined in manifold ways throughout history, yet in modern society it seems we prefer to live as if it didn't actually exist. List some ways in which your view of mortality plays out in your everyday life. Then, create another list of ways in which your life would change if mortality didn't exist. Compare the two lists and discuss what they show you with your group. Where does a Christian response (that death exists but should not be feared) fit into this conversation? Talk with each other about how you feel you could more fully embody the Christian view on mortality.

Activity

Find a movie or book that deals with the issue of mortality. When watching or reading it, think about how the views expressed have been influenced by the overarching view in society as a whole. How would the story change if the author were a believer and viewed death as Christians should view it?

Before You Read Chapter 2

Each and every person reading this book will approach the topic of marriage and relationships within the framework of how they saw their parents handle their marriage. How they have experienced intimate relationships is also a big factor. The tradition of marriage is often housed in a great deal of cultural and social biases that help define how we see it.

As you read Chapter 2, begin to contemplate your present relationship status. Whether married or single, how do you currently see God working in your relationships? Are you able to appreciate where God has you now, or do you find yourself striving to mimic the relationships you see in others?

CHAPTER 2

LIKE A HORSE AND CARRIAGE—MARRIAGE AND THE QLC

"But if you do marry, you have not sinned, and if a betrothed woman marries, she has not sinned. Yet those who marry will have worldly troubles, and I would spare you that."
1 Corinthians 7:28

Introspection

Those of you who are single may be thinking, *This guy is married.* Not only married, he is *happily* married. He has no earthly idea what it is like to be single. I'm sure his advice is really going to be awful.

If that crosses your mind, let me remind you that I have been married only a few years. I'm 29 years old, so do the math: I was single for about 25 years, giving me roughly eight times the experience as a single person that I have had as a married person.

Perhaps it is the married people that should be wary of my advice.

Either way, this chapter's "Introspection" is divided into two parts, one for singles, and one for married people. You're welcome to read both parts, of course, but the stuff in each section will be more applicable to whichever relationship status matches yours.

The issue of relationships in general, and marriage specifically, is a tricky one for someone first entering or already trudging through a QLC. Much of society holds it as part of the idealized life, along with a fruitful career. The concept of a white-picket fence and 2.5 children running around the yard while you and your spouse sip iced tea on the porch swing is what we all need to be happy.

But is it really necessary to be married? Will marriage help you escape the clutches of a serious QLC? Or if you are married, why are you even having a QLC? Shouldn't the realization of a loving spouse be enough to topple any feelings of doubt or depression?

QLC for Singles

Pretend, for a moment, that you just turned twenty years old. (This may be easier for some of you than others, depending on your current age.) Pretend that at age twenty you hear someone describing a man she has just met. She says the person is thirty and single. What are the first images that enter your college-age mind? For many, thoughts immediately turn to an unshaven Neanderthal, in a bathrobe, eating canned chili in his parents' basement – or in a bachelor pad strewn with pizza boxes and unwashed clothes. Perhaps this is a bit exaggerated. But it is not uncommon for our society to stereotype men and women on the basis of their relationship status alone.

Now fast-forward to whatever your actual age is at the moment. For some, perhaps that illustration hits close to home. Embarrassed, you may have just put this book down to throw away your half-eaten can of chili. However, for most of you, this stereotypical description does not suit you in the slightest. Perhaps you are busily climbing the corporate ladder, because, after all, society has told you that to be successful you must be wealthy. Perhaps you have dedicated your life to ministry or service, and as such have not felt the call to be married. Perhaps other external or internal factors have made marriage an impossibility for you at the moment. Whatever the circumstance, why is being single something that must be regularly defended as a legitimate choice in society, while marriage is seen as the norm?

Even today, in many countries, arranged marriages are still common. One description in Japan, where "omiai" (arranged marriage) occurs roughly 30% of the time, speaks of the system like this:

> When a woman reaches the marriageable age of twenty-five, she and her parents compile a packet of information about her, including a photograph of her in a kimono and descriptions of her family background, education, hobbies, accomplishments and interests. Her parents then inquire among their friends and acquaintances to see if anyone knows a man who would be a suitable husband for her.[2]

Perhaps an even more curious aspect of modern relationships is that I cannot point to any society in which a precept of "arranged singleness" exists. I can remember, as a single person, that the external pressures to get hitched were enormous. If you want proof, start dating someone and then take him or her to my grandmother's house for family dinner on a Sunday. Afterwards, you will feel obligated to stop by Home Depot on the trip home and start a wedding registry. The truth is, Western society would have you believe that if you are unhappy and single, then you are probably unhappy *because* you are single.

"But," some of you may be thinking, "I am fine with my lack of a romantic relationship right now. I feel that God is building and preparing me for what is to come, whether that be marriage or not. But, I *do* feel unhappy … and I *am* single …"

The cognitive dissonance you may be experiencing is common. You know in your heart that there are other reasons you are going through a QLC. Your depression may not be in any way related to not having a spouse. But you are bombarded by a society that would have you believe otherwise. Take hope! The Bible has many wise things to convey to those of you who are single.

Others of you may be thinking, "I *know* that my lack of a romantic relationship is what is causing me such heartache. And, on top of what I feel inside, I am constantly being told that being single at my age is out of the ordinary. What is wrong with me?" You, too, must take hope.

For some, God simply has no intention of you finding a mate during your life. This has to be something that you are willing and open to accept. Matthew 19:12 says:

> For there are eunuchs who have been so from birth, and there are eunuchs who have been made eunuchs by others, and there are eunuchs who have made themselves eunuchs for the sake of the kingdom of heaven. Let anyone accept this who can.

The word "eunuch" commonly refers to someone living an unmarried life. What if God so desperately wants your attention and devotion that He is telling you to remain single your whole life just so you can enjoy your relationship with Him to the fullest?

For some of you, God just wants you to be patient, enjoy your life of being single until the time is right to reveal to you the person He has chosen for you. God is always shaping and molding us into more and more of the person He wants us to be when Jesus returns. Perhaps He has not yet shaped you into the person your future spouse needs. Would you rather find that person now, and cause him or her to stumble – or would you rather find that person in God's timing, when you are ready so you can both walk as closely with God together as possible?

Singleness is not viewed in the Bible as substandard to marriage. In fact, singleness provides many unique spiritual opportunities. Yes, marriage was given as a gift from God, and as we discuss more later, it should be seen as an example of Christ's relationship with the church. Also, marriage is provided by God to assist with sexual temptations caused by our sinful natures. However, a person can still be single and rejoice! If you ever need an example of how to be single and successful, just look at Daniel, Jeremiah, Paul...and, of course, Jesus.

In closing this section on singleness, it will be good to read a message from Paul, one of the Bible's happiest bachelors. Paul lived his life as though Christ would return at any moment (as should we). He also lived with as few distractions away from God as possible. Those of you enjoying the gift of singleness, take it as a comfort, at the very least, and perhaps sprinkle some of it into conversation the next time you visit your grandmother:

> I want you to be free from anxieties. The unmarried man is anxious about the affairs of the Lord, how to please the Lord; but the married man is anxious about the affairs of the world, how to please his wife, and his interests are divided. And the unmarried woman and the virgin are anxious about the affairs of the Lord, so that they may be holy in body and spirit; but the married woman is anxious about the affairs of the world, how to please her husband. I say this for your own benefit, not to put any restraint upon you, but to promote good order and unhindered devotion to the Lord. (1 Corinthians 7:32-35)

Married but Still in a QLC

My wife and I have both lived through the life changes that happen when parents divorce. Depending on the age of the child when the split happens, the experience can range from a gradual pain that grows in intensity as the years progress (and our understanding increases), or it can be an all-out, life-shattering trauma. Mine fell somewhere in the middle. My parents were married until the year I turned eighteen. I found out later that they stayed together simply to be there for me until I was able to get out on my own. I felt their love for me growing up, but it was difficult to feel their love for each other. When they decided to divorce after I left for college, I was crushed—not because I thought they belonged together, but because they hadn't done it sooner. I wondered why they would have tortured me my whole life with their fighting only to tear away from each other as soon as I was out the door. It has taken me some time to appreciate the sacrifices they made for me by staying together. Looking back, I could never let my own view of the situation keep me from feeling the love in which they acted for my best interests.

Many of you are in a similar situation. If you fall into the QLC age range, then you were born during a time in our country when divorce rates reached their peak. Those of us born in the West during the 70s and 80s were as likely to have married parents as we were to have divorced parents. And although the divorce rate has dropped slightly, the percentage is remaining stable even now.

For families, the outlook is dismal, to be sure. What can make it even more disturbing is the realization that our views on love, sex, and relationships are entrenched in the view we have of our parents' relationship. A recent sociological study showed that "parents' attitudes toward premarital sex, cohabitation, and being single are strongly linked to those same attitudes among their adult children when parents' marital quality is high than when it is low."[4] Add to these statistics the social pressures placed on marriage in this country, and it is no wonder that fears about the stability of marriage are common during a QLC.

Just as with other aspects of QLC, the issue of marriage can grow out of the dissatisfaction of our childhood and teenage years. Perhaps the "honeymoon" period has worn off in your own marriage. You are both sitting in a small apartment with a growing pile of student-loan bills on your kitchen counter. You long for the days when you used to go on dates after class (paying for them, of course, with your parents' money), the days when you spent at least a half hour prior to seeing that person you were dating just making sure that every aspect of your appearance was optimal. You long for those times as you start to see your spouse as he or she truly is, not as the man or woman of your dreams looks when you are going out to a club or movie. Now you know her when she the first wakes up in the morning, or when he is sick. It dawns on you that this is your life…and you freak out.

Divorce was as much of an issue during the time of the Old Testament as it is today. However, the difference then, as in most ancient societies, including Hebrew culture, was the subordination of women. Men were allowed to divorce women, but women were not granted the same privilege. Also, the list of things for which a man could divorce his wife was vague at best. Deuteronomy 24:1 says "When a man takes a wife and marries her, if then she finds no favor in his eyes because he has found some indecency in her, and he writes her a certificate of divorce and puts it in her hand and sends her out of his house, and she departs out of his house." From this verse, it is clear that it was not just adultery or infidelity that merited divorce in those times. The issue of women's subservience to men in this regard could fill an entire book on its own. However, I want to focus on the idea that divorce could—and did—occur for incidental reasons. Because one gender was so overrepresented in the court of law and the neighborhoods, it was easy to take a lackadaisical approach to divorce.

In this regard, things now are very similar. Marriage is viewed culturally as a contract at best and a game at worst. Rather than devoting your life to another person for as long as you both shall live, society would rather have you think that a marriage should be terminated even on the slightest disagreements. From what we can see in the popular media, with the short duration of many celebrity marriages, the use of prenuptial agreements and the like, it is not difficult to see that our society has a seriously warped view of what it means to be married.

Someone facing a quarter-life transition can be easily daunted by such high standards. If divorce is likely to result from minor disagreements, how could anyone ever hope to stay married? If society tells me that my wife could leave me for something as simple as not folding the bathroom towels correctly, what chance do I have?

We must always remember that society's view rarely aligns with God's view. God sees a marriage as a lifetime commitment. He considers the relationship between a man and wife as a metaphor for the relationship between Christ and the church. If this is how it is, we should be grateful that Christ doesn't take marriage as lightly as our culture does!

Early in our marriage, my wife and I had some struggles. As many young couples can attest, there is a period of transition when you go from living your own life to sharing that life with someone else. You bring certain things of yourself, good and bad, to the relationship. Each of you must learn those things about each other in order to move on together. Through our years together, these differences have sometimes resulted in heated discussions. Additional pressures from the way we view our parents, and from society at large, could increase the agitation. But by dedicating ourselves to each other, and to God as the center of our marriage, we are able to see how these brief agitations carry no weight when we are both focused on the Father's will for our relationship.

God is an ever-present, always-loving stalwart that couples can rely on. He is there for each of us individually and for both of us together. He has our individual and relational needs in mind, and we can rest in His promises that all things work for good if we simply trust in Him. As my wife and I grew together, and as we learned to trust our marriage to God, we made a covenant to each other and Him to never get divorced. Having such a commitment in place not only keeps God central to both of us, it can help make small arguments seem less intense. When you know you will spend your entire life with someone, regardless of their flaws or faults, then coming to terms with how to handle laundry on the floor or an upright toilet seat becomes much easier. Just as God gives us the strength to live our own lives to the fullest, He can give us the strength to make sure our partner has the fullest life possible as well.

In closing this portion of the chapter, I come back to the issue with which it began. You may have divorced parents, or you may be divorced yourself, trying to find the path God has for you following such a difficult change. I have shown the Bible to be explicit in condemning casual divorce. But I hope you leave this topic knowing that, although God does indeed hate divorce, He does not hate divorcees. Just as God wants us to view marriage as a reflection of our relationship with Christ, He wants us to see it as something created to help us feel happy and loved. Part of why He hates divorce is because He hates what it does to the people involved. All sin, from divorce to murder to lying, separates us from communion with God. But just as I know God has forgiven my parents for their divorce (they have both remarried and are closer to Him than ever), I know He can do the same for you.

Interview

It became clear early in the process of securing interviews for this book that God had specific people in mind for each topic. For instance, I interviewed my pastor for the topic of mortality because in him I saw someone who was not only seeking constantly after God's purpose in this life, but who was also strongly in tune with the things God is striving to prepare us for following this life. While prayerfully seeking who to interview for the topic of marriage, I was at first overwhelmed. I was not overwhelmed by a lack of possibilities...but the abundance of them.

Within Christianity, there seem to be more books written on the topic of marriage than anything else. It also strikes me that there are more church conferences on how to make marriage work than there are dedicated to evangelization or missions. But why so much interest in something that is outlined so simply in the Bible? There is quite possibly no other single issue more clearly described in Scripture than marriage.

On second thought, of course, most of us can easily understand why so much time and marketing is spent by churches on keeping marriages together. Quite simply: we see the statistics around us. The ratio of divorces to lasting marriages, both outside and within the church, is terrifying enough to make most anyone reconsider approaching the altar in the first place.

I approached Craig Gross about doing this interview because his ministries are Spirit-driven to circumvent the problems that can crumble a marriage, rather than simply applying salve to relational wounds. He and his staff work diligently to preserve the holiest human relationship outside of our walk with the Lord. They do it by changing people's minds about the true nature of love.

Perhaps most importantly, though, I chose Craig because he is living proof that healthy, godly marriages can prosper in a world that so doubts the possibility. Craig and Jeanette have been married for ten years. In that time, he has written six books, and founded a ministry dedicated to helping people who struggle with the problem of pornography.

But Craig was not simply content to preach against the evils of the porn industry from the comfort of a pulpit. He has a heart seeking the representation of God's love in this world. As a result, he boldly and courageously attacks the root of the problem. To that end, he went to participants in the porn industry to ask some questions. Within days of his initial journey into the porn industry, some people in the church began to condemn Craig's efforts as immoral and ineffective. At the same time, many others affirmed him, opening their hardened and often broken hearts to a relevant and authentic Gospel they hadn't seen from mainstream religion.

The XXXchurch website mixes the seedy with the sacred in an effort to address the generally taboo subject of pornography. In the seven years since it began, XXXchurch.com has had over 70 million visitors to the website and almost a half million people using X3watch Accountability

Software. Craig has been featured in *GQ*, *Good Morning America*, *Newsweek*, CNN, *LA Times*, *Nightline*, *and The New York Times*. His ministry is the subject of an award-winning documentary as well as a new reality TV documentary.

Craig was the man God led me to interview because he has not only dedicated his life to showing others the true meaning of relational love, but he has dedicated his life to showing that same love to his own wife and family. My first impression of Craig was of a man who thrived on action more than words. Although he has authored six books, it is easy to see that he far prefers being in the lion's den to simply writing or talking about it.

Knowing this, I dove quickly into my questions. I wanted to know how someone who regularly encounters broken views of love feels about the current outlook on marriage in society. His experience with families, specifically in how they are influenced by pornography, gives him a feel for the pulse of relationships in America.

So I asked Craig: How do you think marriage is currently viewed in the eyes of society as a whole?

> *I think marriage is seen as a 50/50 proposition at best. I don't think that it is seen at all these days as something permanent. And, ultimately, it boils down to the fact that I don't think enough people realize the work it takes to be in a marriage and to be committed to it.*

This seemed like a grim outlook, to be sure, albeit a commonly-occurring one. But I wondered if a person's view of marriage tends to coincide with his or her religious beliefs. What, I asked Craig, are some of the main differences between how believers perceive a "happy marriage" and how non-believers perceive it?

> *I think one of the biggest differences in how marriage is viewed occurs in the spiritual realm. In a true Christian marriage, not only is the husband the spiritual leader, but God is within the marriage as well, at the center.*

I wondered if Craig felt that singlehood is still seen, societally, as inferior to being married. And, if he did feel that way, why did he think it was the case?

I don't know if it is necessarily inferior. But I do feel that, in general, people just want to get married. Maybe not everyone, but within the society that we live in it is almost expected that you get married. Come to think of it, marriage is like sex in our society. Everyone that isn't doing it wants to be doing it.

I began speaking to Craig about the quarter-life crisis, and its specific challenges. I asked him what he thought were the biggest relationship challenges to people facing their QLC.

I think the single-biggest challenge is just finding someone with whom they want to spend their life. Truly grasping the work that relationships take, the time that must be devoted to that person amongst all other things in their life.

Apart from the challenges of a marriage, how does the spiritual focus of a believer that is single differ from a believer that is married?

I think that when you are single, then that's it … it's just you. You have more time to do all the things required of you. You are the focus. The second that you get married, two people become one person. His or her needs become your needs. It is no longer simply a solo project. It's like the difference between tennis and basketball. One is a team sport and one is a solo sport.

Before concluding the interview, I asked Craig if he had any last words of advice for quarter-lifers currently facing relationship struggles.

The most important thing I can tell you is don't keep secrets. Lay everything out on the table now, not later. This is specifically for people still single but in relationships. It is much easier to back out of a relationship before you get engaged. Figure things out and take your time with it all. Don't rush things simply because of outside pressures. Talk and pray about everything … sex, porn, money, careers. Don't set yourself up to be shocked later … or blindsided.

Inspiration

Jesus has much to say, both with His words and actions, on the unique issues faced by those both single and married. Just as He displays the two seemingly opposite ideologies of grace and truth, He perfectly demonstrates how to live as both single and married. In His message, He offers a guidebook to a holy and sanctified marriage with which no self-help book could ever hope to compete. In His life, He models for us the life of a single saint, fully devoted to His church and His God. As with all other difficult obstacles in our earthly lives, we need simply to follow in His sandaled footsteps in order to find the clearest, most fulfilling route.

Jesus on Singlehood

First, what assistance does Jesus offer the person who is not currently in a romantic relationship? Is being single less desirable than being married? Are people single simply because they are not mature enough to be married?

1. Jesus was single.
The preceding sentence should be enough to answer both of my last two questions. However, let's look further at what Jesus said about being single.

2. Jesus said that being single was a gift.
In Matthew 19, we find another attempt by the Pharisees to back Jesus into a philosophical corner. And, once again, they fail miserably. However, more than the challenge of the Pharisees, this chapter describes Jesus' views on marriage and divorce, which we shall talk about later. The important verses for this section are 10 and 11. After hearing that divorce is a serious violation of God's will for us, and not a simple matter of dissolving a marriage over minor disputes as rabbinical law would have them believe, the disciples were caught off guard. They had been taught their whole lives that something as simple as burning a piece of meat was grounds for immediate divorce. Matthew shows us that: (v. 10) "His disciples said to him, 'If such is the case of a man with his wife, it is better not to marry.'" Look at Jesus' reply: (v. 11) "But he said to them, 'Not everyone can accept this teaching, but only those to whom it is given.'" Celibacy is a gift! This can be exciting for both singles and married people. For singles, it is reassuring to see that perhaps God has blessed you with the gift of celibacy so that

you remain fully devoted to Him. For married people, being single is not in any way better, and does not make the single person "more spiritual" than those who are married. For example, God has blessed some with the gift of preaching, but not all. This does not mean that those of us without the gift of preaching are of any less value in the kingdom. So it is as well with the gift of celibacy. So long as we are using the gifts God has given us, remaining in His will and not our own, we are all different and equally important parts of the Body of Christ.

3. Jesus was single because He wanted to be.
There are some who are experiencing the depression of having not found "the one." Perhaps your family is telling you, in not so many words, that most people your age are married by now. How can I be single and that jerk from high school already has three kids and is in a couples' tennis league?

Had Jesus desired to be married, there would have been opportunity. Many scholars attempt to show, with little evidence, that Jesus was married to Mary Magdalene. This debate remains simply because at the time of Jesus' ministry, it was inconceivable that there would be a celibate rabbi. They were nearly all married. However, as one can easily see by following His ministry, from the houses to the streets to the shores and finally to the cross, that if Jesus were married, His ministry would have been divided.

Sometimes, as singles, it seems that marriage has just been delayed. It can become easy to attempt to search on our own for the right person to marry. Even in doing this, we can easily stray from the path God has for us, the path of righteousness, and the path of ministry. Whether or not you are destined to marry is up to God. Only until you are fully devoted to Him will He fully divulge what He has for you. Ultimately, we must see the possibility of celibacy as something to be welcomed, not a source of shame. As Matthew 19:12 says: "For there are eunuchs who have been so from birth, and there are eunuchs who have been made eunuchs by others, and *there are eunuchs who have made themselves eunuchs for the sake of the kingdom of heaven. Let anyone accept this who can."* (emphasis added)

Jesus on Marriage

As we have already seen, Jesus shattered all of the Jewish paradigms of marriage that had been long tainted by traditions rather than sound doctrine. He reinstated the sanctity of marriage as God had originally intended. For someone who lived a celibate life, Jesus had much to say to those of us that are married. There is some that is uplifting, some that is humbling, but ultimately He gives us a picture that will be fulfilled when He returns to gather up His followers.

1. The tradition of marriage is holy.

The idea that divorce is patently against the original intent God had for a married couple was groundbreaking for many people during Jesus' time – and still is today. Though it has taken on less and less moral severity (perhaps due to the difficulty many pastors are having in their own marriages), God's standard never changes. Matthew 19:8 gives us Jesus' stance on why divorce happens: "He said to them, 'It was because you were so hard-hearted that Moses allowed you to divorce your wives, but at the beginning it was not so.'" This is a clear statement that marriage was designed by God as a lifelong commitment, and a holy institution. In that same chapter of Matthew, verses 4-6, we see that marriage is holy and ordained by God: "He answered, 'Have you not read that the one who made them at the beginning "made them male and female," and said, "For this reason a man shall leave his father and mother and be joined to his wife, and the two shall become one flesh"? So they are no longer two, but one flesh. Therefore what God has joined together, let no one separate.'" Jesus is telling us that God views a married couple as *one flesh*. He tells us that God *Himself* has joined the two in marriage together.

This can be an intense awakening for many in the Christian community. The divorce rate among Christians is basically equal to that of unbelievers. However, let us first realize that God knows that some of His children will become divorced for invalid reasons – just as He knows His children will lie, covet, and any other of the thousands of things we do on a daily basis that fall short of His glory. We should not see this as something about which to be chronically shameful. We should see it as a sober reminder about what we need to avoid in our current marriages. The ideal that God has set in place for us is to enjoy our walk with our spouse and our walk with Him as it is intended. We should see any dissatisfaction or stagnancy as an attack from the enemy designed to lessen the beauty of what God has blessed us with in the gift of marriage.

2. The purpose of marriage is family.

Jesus was not a father. As such, the only "family" members, genetically defined, that we see Him having during His ministry are His mother and brothers. Most scholars believe that since His father Joseph was last mentioned when Jesus was twelve, the older man had died at some point prior to Jesus starting His ministry. Through God's words in the Old Testament, we can see that procreation to further the Kingdom was one of the primary purposes of marriage. We can see that God has ordained procreation in Jeremiah 29:6: "Take wives and have sons and daughters; take wives for your sons, and give your daughters in marriage, that they may bear sons and daughters; multiply there, and do not decrease." He has also given us further guidelines for just how to raise our children in Proverbs 22:6: "Train children in the right way, and when old, they will not stray."

We can see how important it is to raise godly children in a godly marriage by how Jesus interacts with members of His family. It is commonly believed that Jesus' brothers were nonbelievers ("Then he went home; and the crowd came together again, so that they could not even eat. When his family heard it, they went out to restrain him, for people were saying, 'He has gone out of his mind.'" (Mark 3:19b-21); "For not even his brothers believed in him." (John 7:5) They were not present during His ministry, and only His mother was present during His crucifixion. Yet, in their disbelief we can see that the true purpose of having children is to raise them as followers of God. Mark 3:31-35 tells us: "And his mother and his brothers came, and standing outside they sent to him and called him. And a crowd was sitting around him, and they said to him, 'Your mother and your brothers are outside, seeking you.' And he answered them, 'Who are my mother and my brothers?' And looking about at those who sat around him, he said, 'Here are my mother and my brothers! For whoever does the will of God, he is my brother and sister and mother.'" Jesus goes so far as to call those in the crowd who believe Him more His family than His own blood relatives, who were standing outside and believing that He was crazy. Just as God has ordained marriage as the means of populating the earth, we must not forget that it is also ordained as the means of populating the Kingdom.

3. The timeframe of marriage is temporal.

It is comforting for some of us to envision an eternity where we are forever hand-in-hand with our spouse, walking through the New Earth gardens, eating apples, playing with the lions and lambs. Granted, depending on the circumstances, it can sometimes be more comforting for others to realize that marriage is only "till death do us *part*." Marriage, as with all parts of a life where we are striving for God's purpose, can be rewarding and also difficult. Never forget, though, that whatever situation the married couple finds themselves in at this moment, Jesus teaches that marriage is not eternal. Perhaps this is a surprise to you. I assumed it would last forever for most of my life, and even reassured myself during some of the more difficult QLC moments that it was true. Since then, I have come to see that we can rejoice even more in it not being eternal. We must first see marriage as Jesus does.

Some religious leaders, this time Sadducees, were again attempting to trick Jesus by posing a complicated scenario in an effort to have Him contradict Himself and His teaching. Mark 12:19-23 sets up the story: "Teacher, Moses wrote for us that if a man's brother dies and leaves a wife, but leaves no child, the man must take the widow and raise up offspring for his brother. There were seven brothers; the first took a wife, and when he died left no offspring. And the second took her, and died, leaving no offspring. And the third likewise. And the seven left no offspring. Last of all the woman also died. In the resurrection, when they rise again, whose wife will she be? For the seven had her as wife." We used this text previously to highlight some aspects of our Christian afterlife because the Sadducees did not believe in the possibility of resurrection. Looking again at Jesus' response shows us this: (v. 24-25) "Jesus said to them, 'Is this not the reason you are wrong, because you know neither the Scriptures nor the power of God? For when they rise from the dead, they neither marry nor are given in marriage, but are like angels in heaven.'" The phrase "they neither marry nor are given in marriage" is actually repeated in three of the Gospels (Matthew 22:29-30, Mark 12:24-25, and Luke 20:34-36).

So, then, Jesus clearly taught that marriage is not eternal. At first glance, this can be saddening. Joking aside, wouldn't it be refreshing to know that we will spend our eternity with the one we are married to? After all, God ordained the marriage, and it's holy, right?

4. The *parable* of marriage is eternal.

The prospect of a marriage that ends at death can be difficult to grasp. Especially since for those of us facing a QLC, mortality alone is difficult enough to comprehend. How, then, can we rejoice in the fact that a great marriage is not eternal?

We must first realize that marriage is a type of parable. It has been granted as a gift to us from God, as a way to subdue sexual temptations, as a means of procreating, as a way to feel completeness and happiness in this earthly life. Still more importantly, it should be seen as having an eternal aspect as well. Though the connection between spouses formed on this physical, current earth is temporary, it has been created as a model for the ultimate marriage: the eventual union of Christ and The Bride of Christ, the Church.

Marriage is an analogy that will be fulfilled when Jesus returns to gather up His followers. This is described first in Paul's letter to the Ephesians, but most beautifully seen in the vision of John in Revelation. Ephesians 5:23-25: "For the husband is the head of the wife just as Christ is the head of the church, the body of which he is the Savior. Just as the church is subject to Christ, so also wives ought to be subject in everything, to their husbands. Husbands, love your wives, just as Christ loved the church and gave himself up for her." As a society of progressive, forward-thinking people, we can sometimes get bogged down in the often-accused misogynistic tone of this passage. A closer look reveals its amazing intent. Just as a husband and wife are made to be one flesh in God, in the same way, so will the Church and Christ. The husband is not a tyrannical dictator, directing the wife in what to do. Nor are wives told to submit to their husbands blindly, or out of a state of inferiority. There is one body, and the husband (as a representative of Christ) is the directing head. The submission of wives to husbands is out of reverence to Christ, and reflects their trust of Christ. Just as Christ works in unity, cooperation, and submission to God the Father, on behalf of the church, so should the husband work in unity, cooperation, and submission to God the Father, on behalf of his wife. It's sometimes easy, in our culture of tolerance, to forget the true meaning behind why things are the way God has created them. Our feelings on how certain things should be were never a determining factor in how God has decided that they must be. His model of marriage, when examined from a place of humility and openness, is a beautiful portrayal of how things will be for eternity.

Beyond all of this, beyond any discussion of headship and submission, beyond any discussion of being single or married, is the eventual marriage of Christ and the Church. This wedding represents the ultimate culmination of our lives as Christians, and the basis of the model of marriage God has given us as His created humanity. Whatever your current relationship status, whatever those around you are saying, whatever your QLC has caused you to think, or the doubts it has put into your mind, they pale in comparison to the party we are going to have at Christ's return!

I would like to end this chapter with a passage from Revelation. Jesus, in His life of celibacy, offered us guidelines for how to live, single or married. Those guidelines are tailored to prepare us, just as marriage for those of us experiencing it on earth is meant to prepare us, for something more wonderful than our human minds could hope to comprehend. So, when you are confronted by the doubts plaguing you about who you should or should not be with, remember that following God is going to eventually lead us all to the same place … a place with no doubts, no depression, no sadness … and a place where we will all be part of the Bride of Christ.

Revelation 19:5-9: "And from the throne came a voice saying, 'Praise our God, all you his servants, and all who fear him, small and great.' Then I heard what seemed to be the voice of a great multitude, like the sound of many waters and like the sound of mighty thunder-peals, crying out, 'Hallelujah! For the Lord our God the Almighty reigns. Let us rejoice and exult and give him the glory, for the marriage of the Lamb has come, and his bride has made herself ready; to her it has been granted to be clothed with fine linen, bright and pure'— for the fine linen is the righteous deeds of the saints.

And the angel said to me, 'Write this: Blessed are those who are invited to the marriage supper of the Lamb.' And he said to me, 'These are true words of God.'"

Engage

Discussion

Before meeting with your group or partner, review the following questions. Write down your answers. When you meet, be ready to share your responses and listen to others.

1. Why do you think society puts so much pressure on people to be in romantic relationships? How has society's definition of love shaped how you view it?
2. In what ways do society and the Church differ in how they approach the meaning of love?
3. If you are single, what is the most significant thing you have learned about being single from Scripture?
4. If you are married, what is the most significant thing you have learned about being married from Scripture?
5. What are some specific ways that your view of marriage has changed in reading this chapter?

Reflection

This chapter delves into an area of our lives that can far too often be more defined by the world around us than by the God that created marriage. In your small group, divide into single and married groups.

Within the single group, contemplate and discuss the following questions:

1. Does your view of being single align more with Paul or with the world's view? Are you able to see the real benefits being single holds for believers? Explain.
2. If God were to audibly speak to you right now and say that He wants you to be single forever, how would you react?
3. What ways, if at all, would your life change if your relationship status made no difference to you?

Within the marriage group, contemplate and discuss the following questions:

1. If you were to offer your marriage to the world as a representation of the relationship between Christ and the Church, what parts of it would show God to the world?
2. Envision your child is preparing to get married and getting premarital counseling to prepare. How likely would it be for your child to tell the counselor that he or she wants a marriage like his or her parents'?
3. How intentional are you with the time you spend with your spouse?

Activity

Each morning for a week, write down two different ways that your life has changed since you have gotten married (or would change if you were to get married). At the end of the week, go through the list and read it aloud. If you have any bitterness about giving up any of the items, ask God why and pray for Him to remove the bitterness. If you are married, share the list with your spouse, and thank him or her for the sacrifices he or she has made for you.

Before You Read Chapter Three

Within a Western cultural framework, autonomy seems as natural as the pursuit of a stable job and a padded bank account. However for believers, the term as most would define it is, at best, confusing and, at worst, contradictory to our faith.

But what would it look like if we reclaimed the word *autonomy*? What if we took the idea of autonomy, being able to think for ourselves and make decisions without being swayed by the wrong outside forces, and applied it to a Christian framework?

What if autonomy was redefined as a life lived solely for God and the decisions and pursuits He wants for us?

As you read this chapter, think about your own sense of autonomy. How much of your faith, how many of your opinions, are currently held because you were brought up a certain way … and how many are held because you yourself have decided to put them into practice? Deeper still, how much of who you are has been predetermined by the society you live within?

CHAPTER 3

USE THAT FREEDOM—AUTONOMY AND THE QLC

"I am the vine; you are the branches. Whoever abides in me and I in him, he it is that bears much fruit, for apart from me you can do nothing."
John 15:5

Introspection

The "me" in crisis would tell you that there are more things in life that seem great (until you actually have them) than there are things in life that actually *do* end up being great (when you actually have them). I would also tell you that the reason many things seem great on the outside is because we have an insufficient understanding of what they really are.

Take this as an example: When I was in kindergarten, one of my greatest loves was playing video games. This hasn't changed much since then; it just happened to start in kindergarten. I can remember abandoning my spelling homework mid-word in exchange for an hour or two of pixilated glee. As Christmas approached, I would begin to see commercials during my favorite cartoon programming that advertised the next big game. The bright images and excited voiceover served to further melt my already-overstimulated young mind into putty for their advertising hands. I had to have that game.

My wonderful parents heard my plea, and under the Christmas tree that year was the small, squarish package signifying that my dream had come true. The cellophane wrapping did not hit the ground before the game was in and I was transfixed in front of the television.

Much to my chagrin and dismay, the game was not really that good. Sure, I spent a few hours trying to make it fun … but it never, ever came close to the amazement I had felt watching it advertised on television.

Was I so blinded by the blitz of color and excitement of the commercial that such an abomination had actually seemed appealing? Why, despite my previous excitement, was I now ready to abandon the video game in favor of the spelling homework?

Many people experience this same sense of betrayal upon exiting high school. In fact, it is on an even grander scale because the advertising of this experience had been happening your entire life. From infancy, our culture advertises to us the wonders of independence. It is not until college that life is truly experienced. It is not until you are out on your own that you can really form your own beliefs, encounter this world all for yourself. Your parents will help equip you, sure, but the ultimate journey must be taken on your own. Throughout high school, the crux of your peers' conversation often revolved around the premise of "I can't wait to get out of that house and on my own." You felt held back, sheltered, and stifled in your creativity and abilities.

And then, it actually happens. You pack up your parents' minivan, nevermore to be used for soccer Saturdays or sleepover carpools. It now contains the sparse contents of a life on your own, typically gathered by the remnants of your childhood bedroom and supplemented by trips to the local department store's seasonal "freshman" collection. You have graduated!

You arrive, and your dorm contains a metal bunk bed and matching metal desk, as sterile as a hospital room. You attempt to make it your own, putting up the John Belushi poster and the ironic dolphin curtains. You meet your roommate, also brimming with excitement about newfound independence. Your parents kiss you goodbye and leave in the emptied minivan. And you are now here. You are on your own.

Your classes start. You are forced to make your own schedule. Adding to the complexity, it is not simply an academic schedule. You now have to decide when to have social time and how much to allow for it, so your grades don't suffer. You have zero money and must now get a job that does not simply go towards funding your entertainment as it did while your parents paid your rent. It goes towards gas, and food, and clothes. You go to your classes, and find professors so grounded in their opinions and beliefs that you start to question your own. You just always believed what your parents said and were never asked to state why. You start dating more than you ever have, and your parents aren't there to enforce curfews or behavioral expectations. Your relationships with friends are no longer based on the guidelines that your parents have taught you. Your relationship with God is under attack from all sides and you don't understand why you feel so confused.

Much to your chagrin and dismay, being on your own is just not really that great.

I can pinpoint for you the exact time I first made a truly autonomous decision. I can also pinpoint the first time my beliefs came under attack. But looking back, it was these decisions and attacks which burned away the chaff so I could sharpen and repurpose my life with God, for *my* reasons and with *my* convictions. Now looking back, I can see my first autonomous decision was not a groundbreaking act but an arrogant act of rebellion that was altogether unnecessary. What was the decision? It was a painful one.

I got a tattoo.

I had been in the dorm for about three weeks and had called my parents zero times. I was relishing my independence because I had not seen the work it takes to truly live on my own. There was a tattoo shop in town, and I had the remaining fifty bucks my parents had gifted me for food during my first month of school. Needless to say, I ate ramen noodles for three weeks and now have a fifty-dollar Celtic cross forever etched onto my upper back. If anything, getting the tattoo finally prompted me to call and check in on my parents, if only to admit to them that I had gotten the tattoo. In the moment, I thought I was truly stepping out on my own. But, looking back, it had simply been the first groaning of my attempts at autonomy.

The first time my beliefs came under attack was an even more debilitating reminder that I had no clue what it meant to be autonomous. I was in the classroom of an atheist professor. The class was "Intro to Religion." He started the course by telling us eager young freshmen that at least one, if not all, of our most intensely held personal beliefs would be challenged, and probably abandoned, by the end of the course. Little did I know how accurate that statement would turn out to be.

What seemed at first to be an awful experience, having my beliefs put into question, made me realize they were not actually *my* beliefs. I had spent so long relying on the judgments and discretion of my parents in their faith that when it came time for me to use them, they collapsed under the weight of me having never really claimed them as my own. In claiming a belief, you are saying you have wrestled with that belief. You have looked at why it is something you should believe in to the point that, if all else around you were to falter, the belief would hold you up.

Going out on your own for the first time looks great from the outside. If you let the growing pains it causes determine what you get from it, then it will remain only great from outside looking in. However, if you claim the growing pains as necessary to your development, if you use the freedom you have been given to refine your beliefs and practices into the system you need to survive, then becoming autonomous can be a great experience. Maybe it will help to explain what being autonomous really means.

I have come to see that autonomy is not simply independence. Independence, on its own, is simply freedom from the control or restraint of others. That is the idea we see as so wonderful while still under the watchful eye of our parents. Autonomy is the concept that we are truly confronted with upon moving out on our own. The two ideas are sometimes confused, possibly resulting in much of the confusion found in this transition period in our lives.

Autonomy can be defined as the capacity one has to make decisions. At first glance, this seems a simple proposition. I like how burritos taste, and so I have autonomously decided that I am a burrito fan. Yet, delving deeper, I believe that true autonomy is a lifelong practice involving the application of morality, ethics, and empathy, along with a multitude of other things. That it is made even more complex when the person approaching autonomy is a Christian. Eric Berne, noted psychiatrist, wrote that "autonomy is manifested by the release or recovery of three capacities: awareness, spontaneity and intimacy."[3] Whereas independence at its core can be seen as being absent from the control of relationships, autonomy is completely relational. Christians believe we operate under an absolute moral code, given to us by God, and that there is a set of beliefs, also given to us by God, to which we are required to subscribe so that our lives can emulate the life of Jesus Christ.

Many of us, upon leaving our parents and our support group of high school and youth group, find that we were little prepared for the autonomy required of us in the real world. We knew what we believed, because we had believed it our whole life. We knew what we liked. We knew how we felt about a multitude of things. It is not the *what* of our beliefs that goes off to college unprepared. It is the *why*. This lies at the center of many of our struggles with autonomy in the context of our QLC. Most people, upon entering college (and later as they enter the workforce), have never truly identified *why* they act, and why they should or should not believe what they say they believe. Many of them are forced to learn through refinement by fire, by having those beliefs attacked, to see if they are worth keeping.

It is not simply our religious beliefs that make autonomy a lifelong practice. If we are truly seeking autonomy, it becomes integrated into the fabric of who we are. We are not making decisions on our own simply because we can. We are making decisions on our own that are based on the moral code given to us by God and on the expectations we know He desires us to meet. We make decisions about friends based on a thoughtful and prayer-filled consideration of how God would *expect* us to decide. We make relationship choices because we care about God and we care about those God has put into our life. An autonomous life is, therefore, never an independent life.

In our journey of life, we are at some point forced to decide what we believe politically, religiously, culturally, educationally, morally, ethically ... the list goes on indefinitely. Caught living as independent creatures, it would matter little what choice we made because we would only be concerned with how it affected us personally. Living as autonomous creatures, it is of utmost importance what we decide. All areas of our belief system, all areas of our life, are affected by both our relationship with God and our relationship with others. This can be a daunting observation. For some of us, it is this realization which causes the true confusion of autonomy within our QLC. We sincerely do care for others in our lives and truly do want what God has for us. How in the world can I hope to form a structure of beliefs in my life that is accurate in its completeness and empathetic in its capacity to care for those in my life?

It's a challenge, to be sure, to live autonomously. It is also one of our greatest gifts from God. Philosophers throughout the ages have questioned the rationality of free will. Why would a holy God find it necessary to create beings with the capacity for evil? Why not just make all of us love Him innately? Wouldn't that be much, much easier?

Our God is a holy God. Our God is a God who created in us a desire to commune with Him. However without having a capacity for evil, our capacity to desire that which is good would disappear. How could we desire something without the possibility of its opposite? If the only food in the whole world was tacos, and I never even knew of the possibility of burritos, how would I ever come to desire burritos? God, in fact, loved us enough to provide us with the capacity for evil because He wanted us to have the opportunity to choose Him on our own! How great is it to think that the God of the universe, who easily could have made us worshipping robots with no capacity to do anything but serve Him, made us able to realize on our own, in our pitiable human state, that we want nothing more than a relationship with Him. How much greater to think that, though we are created with free will, it is ultimately God's desire for us to come to Him voluntarily. The prophet Ezekiel says in his book: "Say to them, As I live, says the Lord God, I have no pleasure in the death of the wicked, but that the wicked turn from their ways and live; turn back, turn back from your evil ways; for why will you die, O house of Israel?" (Ezekiel 33:11) Not only have we been made in God's image, as creatures not intended to be separate from His presence, we have been given the choice to follow Him because we desire it as much as He desires it for us.

Autonomy is a difficult concept for those of us who have not had the chance to experience it firsthand. It is made even more difficult when society has adopted such a strict, individualistic form of autonomy as its ideal. Looking around at our culture gives the perspective that being autonomous should actually be taken to mean acting only in our interests with little to no concern for others, outside of how they can better us and our situation. In fully claiming the autonomy that God wants for us, to realize we have the ability to choose our beliefs and use them to choose Him, we open the door to a life filled with beliefs which only grow stronger as we age, simply because they are so fundamental and empowering to who we are in Him.

Autonomy is not an easy endeavor. Perhaps the reason many people get so bogged down once they enter college is not because their beliefs are under attack ...but because they feel their *ability to believe* is under attack. Beyond simply being on one's own, there are trials beyond description, unanswerable dilemmas, and the certainty that at some point we will fail in our judgment and fall short of the ideal God has for us. For many of us, the trials faced during college are over just in time for us to face new ones in our career and relationships. But when our autonomy is realized, when we see the strength God gives us to believe and to use those beliefs in the struggles, we can find comfort in the fact that our beliefs (that we've come to own) are there to help us keep our footing. There will always be challenges, and there will always be room to grow and mature ourselves and our opinions. I have found many tough situations along the way for which I could have been better prepared. But, I have also found there is little I would want to change. Though my beliefs were tested, and my ideals were challenged, the ones which emerged through a prayerful relationship with the Father are far closer to what He would have me do than anything I could come up with independently. To me, autonomy is only possible so long as I remain wholeheartedly dependent on my Savior.

My beliefs are far from perfect, just as I am. But this is not what determines my autonomy. Living life as a deliberate walk with God, allowing Him to flow through the decisions I make, I strive for a life filled with the true and accurate autonomy that only He can provide. I am more secure in my complete dependence on Him than I ever thought possible, and my autonomy relies on that security.

Interview

The title has changed throughout the years ..."hippie," "Bohemian," and the most recently-resurrected "hipster"...but the definition of being *counter-cultural* has stayed consistent through the decades. People in these groups, who are typically in their twenties, profess a sense of independence from whatever has been labeled as mainstream, specifically those things of interest to their parents. Merriam-Webster has defined a *hipster* as "a person who is unusually aware of and interested in new and unconventional patterns" and *dictionary.com* calls them people who are "characterized by a strong sense of alienation from most established social activities and relationships."

Thus, it seems clear that there could not be a better person to interview on the subject of autonomy than the man who has been given the title of "insider twenty-something." For a man of just twenty-seven years of age, Brett McCracken knows who he is as a person far more than most people in contemporary society could claim. He has dedicated his working life to forming opinions about things. A graduate of Wheaton College and UCLA, Brett currently works as managing editor for Biola University's *Biola Magazine* and is pursuing a Master's in Theology at Talbot School of Theology. He also regularly writes movie reviews and features for *Christianity Today* as well as contributing frequently to *Relevant* magazine. I found his authorship of movie reviews intriguing. It is one thing to have your own opinion about a movie, as all of our friends are so willing to tell us. It is another to get paid to tell people your opinion and have them rely on it when they choose which movie to see.

If anyone could talk to me about what it means to have autonomy, and how Christian quarter-lifers can hope to conquer the stresses of gaining their autonomy, it would be Brett.

After our brief introductions, we settled in to discuss the issue of autonomy. I first asked Brett about autonomy, specifically as it applies to hipsters. How, if at all, does the culture of hipsters come as a result of developing autonomy in our modern Western society?

> *I think that the hipster culture in general has always been fundamentally an expression of personal autonomy," he said. "Hippies, hipsters, Bohemians…the fundamental underlying theme of being hip or cool is being individual or unencumbered by all of society's prescriptive rules and conventions on how to act and dress and be. It's all about elevating that sense of personal autonomy – individually embodying it in a kind of countercultural way to say 'you can't box me in,' or 'you don't understand me.' 'I will always be what I want to be.' The idea of hipsters is a visual expression of that autonomy, bucking convention, dressing in unorthodox ways, whatever. Whenever you have a democratic society it can provide an opportunity for people to do or be whatever they want to be. Society needs a comfortable affluence level to fuel the machine of hipster culture. It's all about bucking your parents' traditions, an assertion of your own autonomy and personal perspective as opposed to what has been imposed upon you.*

Before we went further, I noted that Brett had hit on something I failed to address. Sometimes, being autonomous is a self-imposed decision. Although there are some of us that have had to develop that autonomy after being thrust into the real world, there are some who have chosen autonomy as a way to rebel. I was curious what Brett's personal definition of autonomy was.

> *Being self-sufficient, being able to call all the shots in your life, not being beholden to anyone else in terms of your identity or path in life.*

That definition sounded unappealing to me. As a Christian, I have chosen to not be self-sufficient. I have little desire to call all the shots in my life, and I am quite comfortably beholden to God. I was beginning to see that the typical definition of autonomy and the one I had assumed are contradictory. In my research, I have found that the societal concept of autonomy seems improbable to coexist within a Christian belief system.

As I said before, I do think Christians can have autonomy of a different sort, starting with the fact that the foundation upon which this autonomy is built is Christ. Society values the individual's autonomy, making decisions completely absent from outside influence. God has built us with the ability to choose for ourselves, but He has also built us with the knowledge to realize we need His help if we want those decisions to be the right decisions in the path He has set for us. I wondered what Brett thought about societal pressures, why in America there is such a huge burden on twenty-somethings to be on their own and successful?

> *America has a uniquely acute pressure to go out on your own ... the house, independence, making your own life. I think it is a part of the American self-made man idea. It has been part of our culture and heritage from day one. We reward individuality. It's much less stigmatized in other cultures to live with your parents even into your thirties.*

So we have a society that mandates success, or at least self-sufficiency, and a God who mandates dependence on Him. Does that mean that there is a greater hope for Christian quarter-lifers than non-Christian quarter-lifers? Does this abandonment to depend on God make the transition into an autonomous adulthood easier? Brett, a self-defined Calvinist in his theology, showed how a dependence on God not only gives us the Ultimate Source to turn to in our times of trouble, but that dependence trickles down into how we interact with the people around us.

> *I think a Christian quarter-lifer has a healthier sense of dependence on others. As a Christian who has grown up in the church, I had the sense that there is something a little off in true autonomy. As Christians we are called to live in a community and care for each other and be each other's support.*

So it is obvious that society's approach to autonomy is flawed. But under this modified, Christian autonomy, how did Brett feel God has allowed him personally to be autonomous?

> *I think he's given me the ability to work well on my own and be motivated in an independent way. I'm thankful that he's given me the drive and ambition to be a self-starter and not to be too*

dependent on what others can do for me as much as what I can do for myself. But ultimately I am dependent on him – and whatever autonomy I think I have is really just him granting me all the blessings and successes I think I earn.

So autonomy, as the world around us sees it, is impossible to achieve and undesirable to strive for as believers?

I feel it's a fallacy to think that full autonomy ever really exists. Because I am Calvinist in my theology, I'm a firm believer in the shaping power of external forces. As a Christian, that is God. For people to claim 100% power over their direction in life is a fallacy.

Inspiration

It can be difficult for us, as sin-filled struggling people, to fathom the possibility that Jesus had free will. How could He have lived an entire life of only choosing the right thing to do when we struggle hundreds of times a day with something as simple as getting angry in traffic? But lest we forget that in His divinity, Jesus can teach us how to make decisions, remember that though Jesus was 100 percent God, He was 100 percent man … and as God and Man, He had free will. Those of us developing our autonomy need look no further than the perfect example of Christ to guide us in our empathy, help us structure our beliefs, and make sure to consider each decision carefully through the perfect lens God provides for us in the Holy Spirit.

In the Bible, the most knowledge that we have of the life of Christ is from the time period during the three years of his rabbinic ministry, when His autonomy was firmly established. The glimpses we *do* have of Him as a child show that His ability to make self-determined decisions existed at a far younger age.

1. Jesus' opinions were never His parents' opinions.

When I was twelve, the most autonomy I exercised was which professional wrestler I should cheer for or which cereal Mom should buy (based on the one with the best toy). However Jesus, at just twelve years old, had already developed a social, political, and emotional autonomy beyond that of most thirty-somethings. We know that, per Jewish custom, each year Joseph and Mary would take Jesus and travel with their community to Jerusalem for Passover. At his twelfth Passover, something different happened following the occasion. Jesus made His first autonomous stance. Luke 2:43 tells us: "When the festival was ended and they started to return, the boy Jesus stayed behind in Jerusalem, but his parents did not know it." Notice it says "Jesus stayed behind." The text could also have easily read "Jesus was left behind," though that would change the story's meaning. You see, Jesus was already establishing the basis of His ministry on earth, as the Son of God and Redeemer, and thus had little time to make decisions based simply on what His parents thought was best for Him. It is, however, interesting to note here that this is not a case of disobedience on the part of Jesus. Disobedience to one's parents is not, and should not be seen as, the beginnings of autonomy. As we will soon see, Jesus was simply doing what His Father in heaven wanted Him to do and was not even considering the fact that His parents had already left. Traditionally, Jewish people traveled long distances in large groups for safety, and so it would have been quite ordinary for Joseph and Mary to simply assume Jesus was with one of their relatives. It took them a day's walk before they even began looking for Him, and they could not return to Jerusalem until three days had passed.

Continuing in the text, we read these words:

> When his parents saw him they were astonished; and his mother said to him, "Child, why have you treated us like this? Look, your father and I have been searching for you in great anxiety." He said to them, "Why were you searching for me? Did you not know that I must be in my Father's house?" But they did not understand what he said to them. (v. 48-50)

Throughout our adolescent and teenage years, we often, parrot our parents' opinions on many different issues, religious, political, or otherwise. Here we see Jesus already knows the Scriptures and His earthly mission so that His parents "did not understand what he said to them." It could be said a flaw in past generations of parenting is that parents taught by dictate rather than example, as in "do as I say, not as I do." I do not necessarily consider this a strict *flaw*. However, it is much better for our children's autonomy and their own future adult autonomy if we allowed them to learn from our *example*. They can learn from what we are doing, see *why* we believe certain things, and recognize the true benefit that they have. Jesus knew He had to be in His Father's house to learn and prepare for His future ministry, not because God forced Him to, but because He saw the example God the Father had set. God was leading the very universe into existence; He was leading the nation of Israel, leading humanity – and so Jesus followed His lead. Luke 2:51 contains a beautiful truth. It says: "Then he went down with them and came to Nazareth, and was obedient to them. His mother treasured all these things in her heart." The text says nothing about Joseph and Mary punishing Jesus for His act. There is no curfew given or toy taken away. Jesus simply sees their example of love in coming to find Him, and in how they cared for Him, and *chooses* to obey them.

Our autonomy may be underdeveloped. We may have had parents who told us to obey them in spite of the fact that we saw little benefit of obedience. We may be out on our own and, because of that lack of understanding, do not know how or even why we should have to develop our own opinions and solutions. In the end, we can look to Jesus and see that the perfect Example – the divine and beautiful Reason to have confidence in our autonomy – is found in our Father.

2. Jesus' pressure was never peer pressure.

As His ministry began, immediately following His baptism, the Bible tells us Jesus went into the wilderness. The text actually tells us in Mark 1:12: "And the Spirit immediately *drove* him out into the wilderness" (emphasis added). He went out there to fast for forty days. During that time, He faced constant attacks from Satan and his pressure to compromise. The pressure Jesus faced in the wilderness is no different from the cultural pressure we face today, and can quite easily result in a loss of confidence, a loss of autonomy, and ultimately a loss of purpose – real issues facing those of us in a QLC.

The first doubting pressure Jesus faced was a questioning of His abilities and also an appeal to His human desires. Matthew 4:3 says: "The tempter came and said to him, 'If you are the Son of God, command these stones to become loaves of bread.'" Jesus' response is an amazing reminder of both the importance of things outside of our human needs and wants and an affirmation of the strength we have to overcome through God. Verse 4 says, "But he answered, 'It is written, "One does not live by bread alone, but by every word that comes from the mouth of God."'"

The second pressure Jesus faces in the wilderness is a challenge to test God, to trust that no matter what decision we make in life, no matter how selfish, He will be there to rescue us from the consequences of our foolishness. Verses 5 and 6 describe the attack, "Then the devil took him to the holy city and placed him on the pinnacle of the temple, saying to him, 'If you are the Son of God, throw yourself down; for it is written, "He will command his angels concerning you," and "On their hands they will bear you up, so that you will not dash your foot against a stone."'"

In our self-centered and narcissistic society, we can be pressured into thinking that, as long as we pray and act like we love God, it really doesn't matter what we do. Again, Jesus reminds Satan that, though God is a God of mercy, He is also a God of justice. Though God offers us the free gift of salvation, it is not a gift to be trivialized or underappreciated. Verse 7 says this: "Jesus said to him, 'Again it is written, "Do not put the Lord your God to the test."'"

The final pressure Jesus faces in the wilderness is perhaps the most common one facing us in today's culture. It is the pressure to be successful and to be in control by taking a short cut. Western society can sometimes seem to not appeal to our sense of autonomy so much as it appeals to our sense of egotism. We are told that, with the right career, or the right spouse, or the right car, or the right jeans, we can be the person we are supposed to be. Matthew 4:8-9 tells us: "Again, the devil took him to a very high mountain and showed him all the kingdoms of the world and their splendor; and he said to him, 'All these I will give you, if you will fall down and worship me.'" The wisdom of Jesus cannot be thwarted, however. He returns with perhaps the simplest, most important truth we can hold. "Jesus said to him, 'Away with you, Satan! For it is written, "Worship the Lord your God, and serve only him."'" (verse 9)

Jesus faced intense pressure in His thirty-something years. His pressure ultimately led to a tortuous evening of prayer in Gethsemane, when He was so distraught over His impending crucifixion He sweat blood. Each and every time, no matter the pressure, Jesus responded by returning to the words of His Father. Whether pressures from culture, pressures from finances, pressures from relationships, or the pressures of facing mortality, not one single human will live their days without facing stressors of some sort. Life will have pressures. Because of the changes occurring in our life at this specific time, the pressures faced during a QLC can be some of the most intense we will ever know in our lives here on earth. However, we need look no further than Jesus' words in John 14:30-31 for a beautiful reminder of how we can not only suffer through those pressures, but overcome them. He says: "I will no longer talk much with you, for the ruler of this world is coming. He has no power over me; but I do as the Father has commanded me, so that the world may know that I love the Father. Rise, let us be on our way."

3. Jesus' convictions came from His confidence in God.

Part of developing true autonomy is not just holding opinions, which can be easily obtained and based on subjective experiences. We must determine our convictions. Whether political, religious, or in any other arena of our lives, convictions are vital in displaying and acting on the beliefs we hold and their importance to us. Also, opinions are just as easy to be changed as they are to obtain. Without firm convictions, the foundation for our morals and ethics, the infrastructure of our most closely-held beliefs, will be built on sand.

We live in an era of relativism. Postmodern thought has told us that any belief is to be valued and accepted, so long as it is true *to the person professing it.* Yet, time and again, we are given glimpses of an objective moral law, which operates independently of whatever anyone one believes about it. We teach our children tolerance and then get angry if our child is pushed on the playground. We are expected to be tolerant of all behaviors at our workplace but still get fired if we are caught stealing from the company. Despite all attempts to subjectify morality and ethics, we cannot be seekers of truth and ignore that morality exists in an absolute sense, given to us by an Absolute Presence. A multitude of apologetic works can be referenced that articulate Christianity's unique worldview on this issue. For now, we will simply fall to the wisdom of G.K. Chesterton on the importance of convictions when he says, "Tolerance is the virtue of the man without convictions."

How then can we hope to hold convictions which truly guide us toward God's path for our lives? When we are entrenched in the mounting pressures of a QLC, how do we separate our truly necessary convictions from the intense push of what society deems important?

Looking to Jesus, we see the most important step in developing a framework of necessary convictions is to remember to *whom* we belong. John 3:35 tells us "the Father loves the Son and has given all things into his hand." In His ministry, Jesus faced intense scrutiny and persecution of his teachings and actions. Without a grounded set of convictions, He could have buckled under the pressure. Despite all the attacks, He remained a stalwart for the message He was sent to deliver. In the adolescence of our own lives, we could oftentimes be rightly charged with mimicking our parents' convictions without questioning their meaning or importance.

During Jesus' ministry, the Pharisees could be accused of the same crime. Their lives were so focused on the rules and traditions of the religion they professed they did things simply because that is how they had always been done, never questioning why. In one exchange, they approached the disciples about eating "with defiled hands" some food from a Gentile market. According to the Jewish elders, Jews were required to wash their hands after shopping at any market employing Gentile workers, to remove any trace of defilement. Ever strong in His convictions, Jesus is quick to point out the true importance of being clean:

> The Pharisees and the scribes asked him, "Why do your disciples not walk according to the tradition of the elders, but eat with defiled hands?" And [Jesus] said to them, "Well did Isaiah prophesy of you hypocrites, as it is written, 'This people honors me with their lips, but their heart is far from me; in vain do they worship me, teaching as doctrines the commandments of men.' You leave the commandment of God and hold to the tradition of men." And he said to them, "You have a fine way of rejecting the commandment of God in order to establish your tradition!" (Mark 7:5-9)

Jesus constantly endured venomous attacks on His most precious beliefs and convictions. At times, it seemed everyone around Him disagreed with His message. We may feel the same way at times. We are Christians in a world of unbelief. We are truth-seekers in a world of relativity. Our attacks may not be as shattering as the ones Jesus faced, but our response should be the same as His if we hope to develop and maintain the convictions God would have us hold. We should never forget we belong to the Creator of truth, the Holder of light, and the ultimate Judge of what is truly good for us and for the world.

4. Jesus' autonomy came from His dependence on God.

Throughout this chapter, I stress the importance of not depending on others to form our convictions, beliefs, or our autonomy. As children, depending solely on our parents' convictions – with no question as to why they are held – can only serve to stunt the growth of our own autonomy when we reach adulthood and are required to develop it. This is not because we are not in a position to question why we believe what we do.

The biggest reason we should not follow the convictions of anyone around us is because, as humans, we are under the control of a sin-filled earthly nature. Thus it follows that, were there Someone to follow who leads us in a perfect example for life apart from sin's influence, it would be wholly and rationally acceptable to base our own convictions on that person's leadership. If the company for whom I worked as led by someone who embezzled, I would probably not be rational in utilizing their model as a basis for my work ethic. However, if the same company offered a philosophically-sound and financially-viable plan by which my job performance could improve, it would make much more sense for me to implement it. In following this business model, it should be noted that, we would not be abandoning our free will. It is our ability to make our own decisions which led us into choosing the prosperous business model. I was not forced to work according to it. Just the same, in developing His autonomy, Jesus recognized the importance of God as a standard by which our behavior and beliefs should be measured. John 5:19 gives us a stunning example of Jesus' dependence on God: "So Jesus said to them, 'Truly, truly, I say to you, the Son can do nothing of his own accord, but only what he sees the Father doing. For whatever the Father does, that the Son does likewise.'" As humans, we have been beautifully designed with free will. Had God wanted to, He could have programmed us to worship Him. He could have forced us not to abandon our pursuit of Him for earthly gain, or turn our backs on Him every time we feel He isn't listening. But a God who created free will would do no such thing. It is in our free will that we can see His goodness. Therefore, though we do have Someone in Whom we can model our convictions, model our beliefs, and model our autonomy, we should remember that autonomy is a chosen lifelong pursuit.

Questioning why our parents believe what they believe is a necessary and viable step on the route towards our own autonomy. Questioning why God tells us to do the things we feel He is telling us to do is necessary and viable as well. However, there is one major difference in the two actions. In questioning our parents, we know that they are imperfect. In questioning their beliefs, we are open to the possibility that not only we are wrong but that they are wrong, because our parents will fail us at times, no matter how hard they try.

In questioning God, however, we can rejoice in realizing that He is perfect. In questioning what He is telling us, we can hope to find our own imperfections, being open to changing our beliefs not because God is wrong, but because we are realizing that our human nature is preventing us from lining up our lives with what God wants for us.

Jesus experienced an evening of torment prior to being arrested. He sweat blood in His turmoil, and all the while His disciples were napping. He questioned what He was supposed to do. He questioned His convictions. I regularly question my own convictions. I doubt my ability to witness, I doubt my life's worth because I see how often I fail. My own QLC caused me to doubt the very love of God that had for so long fueled my love for others.

Ultimately, we are autonomous creatures. We are moral agents, created with the capacity to decide the path of our lives, the friends we have, the job we have, who we vote for, who we marry. The God who made us would have it no other way than this simply because He loves us. He wants our love to be voluntary, never coerced. In gaining autonomy, though, we must remember that we are also fallen creatures. The same free will that can lead us to God has been used by people to walk away from Him, denying His existence and love. This has, in our humanity, resulted in a warped ability to develop convictions and beliefs. We can do it, but only through God's guidance can we hope to outweigh the influence that sin has on us.

Jesus, perfectly God and perfectly human, struggled with the pulls of His earthly nature. As He survived his torturous night in the garden, He prayed three times for God to take the cross away, to change what He had to do. In that moment, His humanity was pushing Him to not go through with it. Except each time, He realized that in order to fully live out not only a life of autonomy, but a life of confident, God-centered autonomy, He must submit. We need only remember seven simple but amazing words. These seven words are a reminder to all of us that we do not have to rely on our own devices to be autonomous. We do not *have* to avoid relying on Someone in our pursuit of personal convictions. We can always count on God, and we can always count on Him having our best interests in mind. The words?

"Not my will but yours be done" (Luke 22:42b).

Engage

Discussion

Before meeting with your group or partner, review the following questions. Write down your answers as well. When you meet, be ready to share your answers and listen to others.

1. How would you have defined "autonomy" prior to reading this chapter? How has that definition changed?
2. Why do you think it is possible to be both autonomous and fully reliant on God?
3. What are the biggest difficulties to developing personal opinions in our current culture?
4. How was Jesus autonomous? In what ways could you be more autonomous?
5. What do you think, more or less, is the most important reason for us to pursue autonomy as believers?

Reflection

In this chapter, we begin to examine how we can best begin the process of building our own beliefs, beliefs free not from God or His influences, but from a society that has a focus opposite God's for our lives. Reflect on the following questions.

1. Why does God's view of our free will look so different from the world's?
2. If you were to order your beliefs from most to least autonomous, what one belief do you hold most strongly as an individual?
3. Are there any beliefs in your life that you still hold simply because your parents held them?

Create a definition as a group of autonomy as it applies to believers.

Activity

Write a letter to God. Thank Him for blessing you with the ability to choose. List some specific examples of beliefs He has developed within you that you are now able to hold autonomously. Write any beliefs that you still hold onto because others hold onto them. Ask God to show you which, if any, you should keep. Write down your reasons why.

Before You Read Chapter Four

Dealing with finances is perhaps one of the most foreign aspects of entering adulthood. As a child, the closest we typically get is making sure that we don't waste our allowance or babysitting money. What does it look like, then, to not only learn how to handle our own finances independently, but do it in a way that glorifies God?

How can something that seems so consuming to the rest of society be embraced and celebrated in the lives of people that follow Jesus?

More so, how can we approach the issue in order to show others how misconstrued and wasted a life lived focusing on money can be?

As you read this chapter, consider how you currently view your own financial situation. Is money something you would say you worry about too much? Is it something you don't think about enough? Where does God fit in when you pay your bills?

CHAPTER 4

SPARE THE PIGGY BANK—FINANCES AND THE QLC

"And he said to them, 'Take care, and be on your guard against all covetousness, for one's life does not consist in the abundance of his possessions.'"
Luke 12:15

Introspection

I judge the quality of the jobs I have held by the uniform (or lack thereof) I was required to wear. For instance, I remember fondly a bright turquoise and white pinstripe dress shirt under an equally-bright turquoise vest, paired with black slacks and skid-resistant black sneakers. This highlight belongs to my first job: grocery store bagger. From there, I progressed into wearing a purple polo shirt along with a black tennis visor and matching black slacks, along with the same skid-resistant black sneakers. These were from my second job as a pizza delivery boy. Following these were a steady stream of nametags, embroidered and collared shirts, and pressed slacks. The shoes varied a bit, from black to brown, yet they each protected me from all forms of skidding. Add to the uniforms the scents and stains that accompanied them following my shift and you can trace a job history winding from grocery store to pizza shop to steak house to bar to country club … all prior to graduating from high school.

You would think after following such a prestigious career path at such an early age, I would have quite a little nest egg waiting for me when I finally got out of college. And yet, upon entering the real world, all I had to show for my years of trouble were an impressive movie collection and a disturbing amount of ironic t-shirts. (So I guess I can't exactly say I had *nothing* to show for it.)

Throughout my years in high school, and even during college, the concept of supporting myself economically was entirely foreign. Sure, if I didn't work I may be unable to go to the movies *three* times in one week. However this was really the extent of my suffering. My parents graciously funded my food and lodging, as they tend to do for their children, until I was of the age where I could take this on myself. Holding a college degree in my hand was a signal that I should have been ready. And so, I set out to brave the real world on my own when I left college, degree in my backpack and résumé in my hands.

I went out, as many do, with dreams of securing a job in the career written on my degree: Psychology. I returned home with a job at a coffee shop making eight dollars an hour. Jaded and bitter, I knew I was settling. I knew I could do better than a coffee shop. Didn't I already survive enough jobs where I had to wear my name on my shirt? Didn't I pay my dues? Is this degree really meant to be mounted only on my refrigerator?

This situation is all-too-common, especially in today's economy. A college degree, previously a sign of intellect and status, no longer holds the merit it once did for prospective employers. There is simply far too much financial aid available to pass up a college education, and more and more people are emerging from four-year programs with undergraduate degrees loaned in full by the government. However, those wonderful moments of grabbing all your textbooks, along with several new pairs of pajama pants, a mini-refrigerator, a ping-pong table, and God-knows-what-else on the government's dime quickly turn to sighs of dismay and grief when that first student loan bill arrives in the mail following graduation. The average student exiting a four-year bachelor's program with a degree owes about $24,000 in student loans. Those simply cannot get paid back very quickly on an eight dollar an hour job. This figure does not even take into account credit cards, notoriously easy to get for college students.

Because it is the more common scenario, much of this chapter will address those of us in the category of "having debt." If you happen to fall into the category of "not having debt"... could you spare a few bucks for an aspiring author? In all seriousness, how can those with a mound of debt hope to not drown in it? How, more importantly, can we keep our focus on God while keeping the lenders happy and attempting to gain some semblance of a financially prosperous life?

First, I must confess that this is not a guide to financial freedom. Honestly, my wife is in charge of our budget, and our life is much simpler and happier that way. I am quite frankly not the person you need to talk to about specific economic advice, unless you want me to pick whether you should get Batman or Superman checks. I do, however, have much to say about how best to overcome the spiritual and emotional trauma financial decisions can cause. While practical economic advice is helpful, if you are not equipped with the ability to deal with what finances can bring about in your spiritual life, you will always have difficulty in this area, no matter how well-off you are. If left to our own earthly devices, human greed dictates we will always strive for a better financial situation … and always come up short.

For those currently suffering financial troubles after college, the issue of where to begin protecting ourselves from financial crisis must be approached by admitting that there is a debt we owe. For monetary loans, there are some options available – such as deferment and forbearance – that dangle the carrot of procrastination in front of us. Yet, even if we utilize these options out of necessity, we must never forget that the debt is still there. We chose to borrow, the cost was weighed, and we must pay it back. And so, we must ask ourselves if it was worth it. Part of why we need ask this is because, especially if we are not quite in a place of having that lifelong career yet, we may feel that we have wasted the money.

The Bible bluntly warns of the trouble that can be caused by borrowing money. Proverbs 22:7 says: "The rich rule over the poor, and the borrower is the slave of the lender." You hear this verse, and then think about that box of movies in your closet or that mini-refrigerator that is now holding extra sodas in your garage and wonder how much less your monthly payment would be had you not obtained them. The point here is not that you are to feel like you are being punished for borrowing money. It is more that, in regard to student loans, you are to remember that because it was borrowed, you now have an obligation – and a spiritual one as a Christians – to repay it. It is of no use beating yourself up over money wasted. You are here now, and just as God has made us stewards with all things He has blessed us with in this life, you are to be a steward with your loans as well. One of the worries of the QLC is that you will never emerge debt-free from your student loans. But with God's help, you can overcome and conquer. In the meantime those mounds of student loans can be a beautiful example of our mounds of sin, and can remind us of how we are helpless to remove those without God as well.

It is beautiful to be reminded of our gift of eternity and how God has written us a blank check to cover our spiritual debts if we believe in Him as our Heavenly Father. I do understand, however, that this illustration could fall on deaf ears when, in the here and now, you find yourself using credit cards to pay for lunch meat. You may know, beyond a shadow of a doubt, that God has forgiven you and is watching over you, but you still have responsibilities. How can we trust in God's providence while making sure to do our part to remove the stress of finances?

Ramen noodles are magical.

Did you know that, though they currently sell for only about twenty-five cents each, there are ten billion dollar's worth of ramen noodles sold annually? They come in meat, mushroom, vegetable, even seafood flavors… each one delicious. I say this to begin a brief discussion on how to be frugal.

Prior to marrying an amazing chef and baker, I learned to love all flavors of ramen noodles. This was not part of some secret celebrity diet plan; it was not at all healthy (considering the amount of salt I was consuming), but it did help to kick-start my path towards being financially stable. Along with cutting back on other things, such as buying less expensive clothes, I pledged to make a purposeful effort to regain my footing. I did this, in part, because I realized how much I squandered those resources in college, taking them for granted. I think part of why we do this as college students is because we are used to the comforts and pleasures afforded to us while under our parents' roof. Many of us grow up and may never once see our parents struggle financially. We have all the food we can eat, all the clothes we could need, and never once have to sit and balance a checkbook. However, ask our parents if it was as seamless as it appeared to be and they would more times than not say it was a struggle. It may be easier for them, because they both have had more practice and have had more years to become established financially. For people just entering the world of fending for one's self, the prospect of living comfortably may seem too far off to be possible. Yet it is in those initial choices, eating in more than eating out, and wearing that second-hand or off-brand t-shirt, where you can begin to pursue a life of balance, a life of stability, and a life for your children to enjoy one day.

Ultimately, you must return your focus to the One from whom we have been given all things. Focusing too much on money, whether in your lack of it or your abundance of it, can cause you to lose focus on God. Luke 16:13 says plainly: "No slave can serve two masters; for a slave will either hate the one and love the other, or be devoted to the one and despise the other. You cannot serve God and wealth." You can just as easily fall into serving money as your master by constantly focusing on your debt, as you can serve it by focusing on being wealthy.

As I mentioned earlier, one must remember that money is a necessary evil in this life. You may very well have debts to pay back; you most certainly have bills to pay. Yet, in having these realizations, you must not forget that your goal from God is not to accumulate wealth … it is to be a good steward of the money you have. That same chapter of Luke, just two verses earlier, tells us, "Whoever is faithful in a very little is faithful also in much; and whoever is dishonest in a very little is dishonest also in much. If then you have not been faithful with the dishonest wealth, who will entrust to you the true riches?"

You may not easily fall into a pattern of trusting God in the area of finance right now. Seeing those bills pile up can be quite an obstacle to faith. How can we hope to trust God with no obvious signs that the problem is going away? We can just start acting like we trust God. As Christians, we are certainly guaranteed to have times where God seems farther away. Our faith will be tested, and though we may not want to admit it, some of our toughest tests of faith can happen around the issues of finance. It is an ever-present, tangible hurdle to an otherwise spiritually-prosperous life.

Psychiatrist David Burns notes that it is easier to act one's way into a new way of believing than to believe one's way into a new way of acting. As you enter this new phase of life in a generation holding unprecedented amounts of debt and a low amount of job placements, your faith could very easily be the first thing abandoned. Mine was brutally tested. Do I really have to eat these noodles for the rest of my life? Am I stuck in this coffee shop as a career?

But slowly, gently, my actions started to change. I started to appreciate the fact that I had a job at all. I started to see my twenty-five cent meals as a sort of restitution for all the dinners out I was able to enjoy during college. I started to use my small salary to whittle at those bills, making myself more and more the type of steward I feel God wants us to be. And now, looking back, I see how my faith was strengthened. Because of my job at the coffee shop, I got the job I never thought possible (more in the next chapter). Because I saved so much money eating cheap, I was able to purchase the car that led me to the place where I would meet my wife.

In the end, I realized that finances should never, ever get in the way of the life God wants for us. They simply aren't important enough. That isn't to say you are to abandon balancing your check book or live Thoreau's life of minimalism. It just means that, as children of the universe's Creator, our lives have a larger focus and a grander purpose than economics. If we trust God with the big things in our lives, we can rest comfortably knowing He will guide us through the smaller things.

Interview

With a topic so prevalent and consuming as finance, and one in which there is such a diversity of opinion, I naively thought finding someone to interview might be difficult. However, that was not the case. I was able to interview someone who is not only connected to Dave Ramsey, one of the biggest names in financial security today… but is also a hilarious guy.

His name is Jon Acuff, and he wrote the books *Stuff Christians Like* and *Quitter*. If you haven't had the chance, I would recommend going right now, no matter what else you have going on, and purchasing those books. Actually, I would not at all be offended if you put this book down for a while to read that one, so long as you come back and finish this one. He has a gift for satire, which as we all know can point serious fingers at things which deserve being examined for change.

He has also written a book entitled *Gazelles, Baby Steps and 37 other things Dave Ramsey Taught me about Debt*. In it, he explores with wit and humor many of the financial issues plaguing our society, softening the edges on an issue that can often brutalize people. I was curious what his perspective on finance would be, specifically as it relates to people in their quarter-life years.

My first question directly addressed what Jon feels the believer's specific purpose is when approaching finances.

> *I believe that we're called to be stewards. Money is an important topic in the Bible and there are lots of verses to reference, but one of my favorites is the story of the way the servants handle the master's finances in Matthew 25. I look at my money, not as something that is mine, but rather as something I have been entrusted with from God. Entrusted to steward and use for the purposes of his kingdom.*

In our culture faced with so many financial pressures, it is refreshing to see a group like Dave Ramsey's that can simultaneously handle economic issues while maintaining God as their real focus. What made Jon Acuff decide to go from simply analyzing Christianity at large to being a part of such a directed initiative?

I wanted to join a company that was active in the general marketplace but still focused and dedicated to the Gospel. The most rewarding part of the job has been learning from that environment. For years and years, the Dave Ramsey team has successfully and humbly grown their company. I've loved learning about how they did it and more importantly, why they did it.

As someone working from within a finance-based ministry, it could be easy to lose focus of the real, practical issues people are dealing with on a daily basis. I was curious, then, of what Jon would say to someone dealing directly with financial difficulties.

I think the biggest thing I'd say is that money is an issue everyone eventually deals with; the problem is that we often don't deal with it until it's a crisis. The more you can proactively take control of your money, work on your debt, and plan for the future, the more you can do what God calls us all to do: give. I'm certainly biased given I work with Dave Ramsey, but more than five years before joining his team, my wife and I read his book, The Total Money Makeover. That book not only changed the way we handle money but also changed the way we communicated as a married couple. I can't recommend that book enough.

It is fascinating to me that people like Dave Ramsey have become such household names. It seems such a recent development for people to be so connected to the minutia of their finances. Have we gotten better or worse at financial planning? I asked Jon how he felt our society has changed its focus on finance in the past twenty years.

I think impatience is one of the biggest issues we face when it comes to money. We have an expectation of something we deserve or feel entitled to and we want it right now. Instead of working slowly and patiently, we demand something right away. For instance, when I was right out of college I bought a mountain bike with a loan. Who gets a loan on a mountain bike? It was ridiculous, but I wanted that mountain bike. And I didn't have the patience to save up for it slowly. So when I got married my wife looked at this weird loan payment I had and said, "What's this?" I replied, "Oh, that's the payment for my mountain bike."

> *Had I saved for it and purchased it with cash I could have bought a nice bike. Instead I paid $750 for a bike that only had a price tag of $500. That's a small example but the consequences of impatience are multiplied when you are apply them to things like cars or houses or large items."*

This discussion was turning out to be a far cry from the sarcasm and blunt humor I was used to from reading Jon's previous book. God has used that book for its own purpose. But it was amazing to see someone shift his life mission, even if just a bit, to more fully align with God's purpose. I feel Jon has done just that. My last question for him was what he felt was the biggest issue of finance facing people of our age specifically. His answer lies at the root of much of our financial struggle.

> *I would say impatience and vanity. We want the things that took our parents forty years to achieve, right now. And with the increase of media and the ability to measure our self-worth in a million new ways (Number of Twitter followers, blog post comments, etc.) it's easy to get wrapped up in trying to maintain our image.*

Inspiration

Jesus' ministry was one of great amounts of action, and somewhat smaller amounts of speaking. He showed us how to live not merely by what He said, but by how He lived. This is unique to Christianity in many respects. Jesus did not lead with a sword; He led with the simple message of love. He did not renounce the world to escape evil; He offered a way for us to be cleansed of it.

He did not offer a quick way to prosper; He warned of the evils wealth can bring.

How, then, in the world of today with its economic pressures and hedonistic lifestyles, can we utilize Christ's message and hope to emerge from a QLC that includes financial stress? It is, perhaps, in what Christ *did not* do that we can find a path towards what *to* do.

1. Jesus was a preacher, not a televangelist.
A September, 2006 issue of TIME magazine appears with the headline "Does God Want You To Be Rich?" The book *Prosperity: The Choice Is Yours* by Kenneth Copeland sits on Christian bookshelves. While an 800 number flashes on the bottom of the screen asking for donations, preachers on television quote Deuteronomy 8:18 with fervor: "But remember the Lord your God, for it is he who gives you power to get wealth, so that he may confirm his covenant that he swore to your ancestors, as he is doing today."

Meanwhile, a simple Son of a carpenter travels with twelve jobless men in rugged sandals telling people to sell all they have and give the money to the poor, so they can have treasures in heaven (Luke 18:22).

Something has changed in the message from Galilee to here.

Prior to the economic downfall of the past few years, prosperity theology became quite popular, mainly in America's Pentecostal churches. Its basic tenants describe a gospel in which God provides material wealth to those whom He favors. Unfortunately, as the real estate market hit all-time lows and banks began closing, prosperity pastors became strangely quiet. A system that professes riches coming to those who have faith in God and struggles for those who do not cannot survive the mirror of truth when an entire economic system collapses. Believers and nonbelievers alike became impoverished.

Jesus did not preach a prosperity gospel. He did not offer people riches in exchange for donations. He did not say the Christian life would be easy or prosperous. Yet what He did say can far better withstand the pressure of an economic crisis than any other ideology.

Luke 16 tells Jesus' parable of a rich landlord. This parable is one of Jesus' more confusing tales, yet it provides an enormous amount of insight into how best to respond to the pressures of finance.

Jesus reminds us that we should be managers of what we have rather than owners:

> He also said to the disciples, "There was a rich man who had a manager, and charges were brought to him that this man was wasting his possessions. And he called him and said to him, 'What is this that I hear about you? Turn in the account of your management, for you can no longer be manager.'" (Luke 16:1-2)

He then shows us we should not only realize what really matters in this life, but that we should use that focus to become knowledgeable about the important things:

> And the manager said to himself, "What shall I do, since my master is taking the management away from me? I am not strong enough to dig, and I am ashamed to beg. I have decided what to do, so that when I am removed from management, people may receive me into their houses." So, summoning his master's debtors one by one, he said to the first, "How much do you owe my master?" He said, "A hundred measures of oil." He said to him, "Take your bill, and sit down quickly and write fifty." Then he said to another, "And how much do you owe?" He said, "A hundred measures of wheat." He said to him, "Take your bill, and write eighty." The master commended the dishonest manager for his shrewdness. For the sons of this world are more shrewd in dealing with their own generation than the sons of light. And I tell you, make friends for yourselves by means of unrighteous wealth, so that when it fails they may receive you into the eternal dwellings. (Luke 16:3-9).

He goes on to remind us that we should be trustworthy and honest with what we do have, no matter whether it is a lot or a little:

> One who is faithful in a very little is also faithful in much, and one who is dishonest in a very little is also dishonest in much. If then you have not been faithful in the unrighteous wealth, who will entrust to you the true riches? And if you have not been faithful in that which is another's, who will give you that which is your own? (Luke 16:10-12)

He tells us we should carefully choose what or who we are to serve: "No servant can serve two masters, for either he will hate the one and love the other, or he will be devoted to the one and despise the other. You cannot serve God and money." (Luke 16:13) Then He finally goes on to tell us we should only value what God values.

This last point, that we are to value what God values, is polemical to the prosperity gospel. Luke 16:14-15 says this: "The Pharisees, who were lovers of money, heard all this, and they ridiculed him. So he said to them, 'You are those who justify yourselves in the sight of others; but God knows your hearts; for what is prized by human beings is an abomination in the sight of God.'" It is little wonder that, during difficult economic times, many who previously put their sincere faith in the prosperity gospel are now wondering where God is in their trouble.

Jesus came to show us the way back to God. He offered a hope that is stronger than any financial crisis. Prosperity gospel shows us the way to money. It offers a temporary respite in a temporary world. One can heal us of our pain and struggle; one can anesthetize them. Which master do you want to serve?

2. Jesus was a teacher, not an entrepreneur.

It is common, especially in Western culture, to feel the need to sell anything that one is talented at doing. Learn to build web pages in your spare time? Then start charging small businesses fifty bucks an hour for your consulting services. Make a wallet completely out of duct tape? Market the idea to hardware stores and they start selling them for an 800% profit. Write papers in high school? Turn that talent into a Christian living book on quarter-life crises.

Why does modern society so impress upon us the importance of getting paid for our services? Jesus' career as a public speaker did not include personal assistants or booking agents. Perhaps part of our dismay at the prospect of looming financial stress comes from our environment being centered on money as a signpost for talent. Yet the man who most people would say was the world's most popular public speaker not only worked for free, He sometimes provided the refreshments.

As quarter-lifers in this generation, we are faced with many daunting statistics. We are the first generation predicted to make less than the previous generation. Among our age group, average earnings are at an all-time low. Thirty-nine percent of students with loans graduate with "unmanageable debt." Add to this the pressures from society, and it is easy to get caught in the appeal to market every possible talent we have for the most money possible.

In His parable of the talents, Jesus gives the example of a master giving his slaves talents, each talent equal to about 20-years'-worth of wages. Taken at face value, this parable seems to be about how to best use the money we are given. Yet, there is a spiritual application as well. Seeing the talents as each worth 20-years'-worth of work, one can make the connection that each talent represents an actual talent, or gift from God, that these people have been given. Just as in the parable one man is given five talents, one two, and one a single talent, people too can have a wide range of talents given to them by God: social skills, athletic ability, intellectual aptitude, musical ability, or any multitude of things. However just as God has given us our natural and spiritual talents, He is the one who has given us our wealth as well. In the Bible we are not instructed to use those talents to make money. We are instructed to use those talents in the service of God and others.

Jesus tells us that the man who received one talent went and buried it, instead of using it in service. In essence, he decided that since he had not been blessed by much, it was his responsibility to make sure he held on to what he had. God does not want us to do this. We are instructed to use our talents, our money, and our gifts in service to God and others. Focusing on our talents as a way to make money not only claims the talents as being our own, it makes the arrogant statement that we deserve the rewards that come from a talent God has given us. In Matthew 25:30, the last verse of this parable, Jesus describes the end faced by the ones who do not use their God-given talent in service: "And cast the worthless servant into the outer darkness. In that place there will be weeping and gnashing of teeth."

The book *In His Steps* by Charles Sheldon, published in 1896, describes an upper-class Protestant church and its members. One member, Rachel Winslow, was blessed with an amazing singing voice. Yet, when given the chance to tour and sing professionally, she turned it down in order to continue singing for free at the church. In response to her mother, who was furious at her decision, she said, "I am hungry to suffer for something.... How much have we denied ourselves or given of our personal ease and pleasure to bless the place in which we live or imitate the life of the Savior of the world?"

Perhaps you have been blessed with many talents or much wealth. In that case, you have an even greater responsibility in the service of God. Jesus says in Luke 12:48: "From everyone to whom much has been given, much will be required; and from one to whom much has been entrusted, even more will be demanded." Perhaps you are in a state of financial burden, trying to regain control of your finances with a world telling you that money solves problems. To that, Jesus responds with perfect wisdom about how trusting in God can bring peace, even from financial suffering. It isn't in the form of a financial seminar, or a five-step way to earn $673 per hour placing small classified ads from home. It is a simple sentence that reminds us of where our focus should always lay.

"But strive first for the kingdom of God and his righteousness, and all these things will be given to you as well." (Matthew 6:33)

3. Jesus was a healer, not a loan officer.

In the Bible, there are twenty-six directly documented cases of Jesus healing people of physical ailments. There are seven exorcisms, three resuscitations of dead people, and crowds of people whom Jesus healed.

In many churches today, we are told that Jesus can heal us from financial troubles. We are told that, if we are faithful and pray, Jesus will bless us with wealth. Though in looking through the Bible, with all of the healings Jesus performed, the number of times He healed someone from poverty amounts to a resounding zero.

As a carpenter, Joseph raised Jesus in the lower end of Nazareth's peasant class. In the time of Jesus' life, Jews were particularly impoverished because not only were they taxed a 3 percent land tax, a 12 percent crop tax, and various other custom, toll and tribute taxes by the Roman government, they were required to offer a 20 percent tithe of their agricultural income to the Jewish authorities. That results in about 35 percent of their income going directly to the authorities. Jesus' upbringing meant He came directly from one of the poorer families in Galilee. Jesus was a poor man preaching to poor people. His ministry never even took Him to the larger cities within Galilee, such as Sepphoris and Tiberias, even though the density of these cities would have made more sense from a strategic viewpoint. Why was it this way? Jesus could have simply asked the Father for any and all the kingdoms of the world. He could have said a word, and all wealth imaginable could have been His.

Yet this is not what He did. He spent His ministry among the poverty-stricken hamlets of the area, where people with no money and great sickness were searching for a way out. However, it is not simply because they were searching that Jesus focused His energy on these places. It is because the people in these places, with their lack of wealth, represent each of us. We may not all be financially poor, yet we are all morally bankrupt. Jesus approached the poor, and rather than offer them the temporary help money would provide them, He offered them treasures in Heaven. He showed them the importance of the riches of God. Matthew 6:19-21 shows us how He described the riches of earth compared to the riches of heaven: "Do not lay up for yourselves treasures on earth, where moth and rust destroy and where thieves break in and steal, but lay up for yourselves treasures in heaven, where neither moth nor rust destroys and where thieves do not break in and steal. For where your treasure is, there your heart will be also."

As Christians, we are instructed to trust the Lord with all things. We are told that, through prayer, all of our needs will be met. It seems logical, then, that our financial needs should be met as well. This may always be the case. I know many people who have had their every financial need met through prayer and faith. Yet, through the ministry of Christ we must remember that having our earthly troubles taken care of should never take priority to having our spiritual needs met. In speaking with the Samaritan woman at the well, Jesus offers a beautiful example of how temporary the things of this earth are in comparison to the things of God. John 4:13-14 says: "Jesus said to her, 'Everyone who drinks of this water will be thirsty again, but those who drink of the water that I will give them will never be thirsty. The water that I will give will become in them a spring of water gushing up to eternal life.'"

Jesus was raised with little in the way of financial wealth. His ministry was spent relating to people who oftentimes had even less than He did. He didn't pay His disciples for their work, nor did He ever offer money to assist people in their troubles. This can leave us one of two ways. We can look around us, see the bills that need to be paid, and get angry with God when He doesn't simply make them disappear, even in the midst of intense prayer and longing. Or, we can look around us, see the bills needing to be paid, and rejoice in the fact that these troubles are temporary. The stresses of this life, financial and otherwise, are all fully understood by Jesus Christ. We are called to be stewards of what we have, to a life of trying our best to take care of the things for which God has put us in charge. More importantly, we are called to a life of focusing on those things that "neither moth nor rust consume."

Perhaps your finances are causing you difficulty in focusing on your walk with God. Perhaps you are finding it hard to trust in a Savior that could say a word and remove all of your debt but doesn't.

Perhaps you should be like the people directly in the path of Jesus' ministry. They had nothing, sometimes not even food or clothes. Yet when Jesus approached them, He didn't tell them to believe and then their debts would be removed. He told them how they might find rest. It is not in finding a way to get rid of our troubles that we can rest in God. It is in trusting them to Him, knowing that the kingdom He offers is one in which our very souls can be at peace.

Financial troubles are something we may all have to face at some point in our lifetime. They may not disappear through prayer, no matter how earnest. Shifting our view to the restful kingdom which is our promise in the Lord can offer us the chance to survive these temporary trials, and even strengthen our faith through them.

"Come to me, all who labor and are heavy laden, and I will give you rest. Take my yoke upon you, and learn from me, for I am gentle and lowly in heart, and you will find rest for your souls. For my yoke is easy, and my burden is light." (Matthew 11:28-30)

4. Jesus was a Savior, not a financial planner.

In a book about how best to handle the tumultuous period of quarter-life, this chapter may stand out as having described many ways of how *not* to handle struggles in the area of finances. Jesus taught us how we should *not* focus on earthly things like money but rather focus on heavenly, eternal things. He taught us how *not* to use the gifts we have been given for personal gain, but rather to use them for the service of God and others. He taught us how *not* to focus on the healing of our financial debt, but rather focus on the healing of our souls.

Throughout this chapter, we see that Jesus wants us to find rest. He wants us to remain peaceful and stress-free in all areas of our life. In other words, He sincerely desires to save us from our earthly troubles. He never tells us that those troubles will disappear. In fact, Jesus promises us we will have troubles in this life. He tells us in John 16:33: "I have said these things to you, that in me you may have peace. In the world you will have tribulation. But take heart; I have overcome the world."

Sometimes, in our darkest hours of stress, depression, loneliness, or anger we wonder why God is letting these things happen to us. "I am a Christian!" we say, "I shouldn't have to worry about this kind of thing!" However, in a way, we *should* have to face those things, and head-on. We deal with them through faith by allowing God to make us more and more into the people He wants us to be. Keep in mind, our earthly troubles are a result of us allowing sin to enter the world and separate us from the perfect, trouble-free communion we could have with God.

Sin tainted us and the world around us. Paul tells us in Romans 8:22-23: "For we know that the whole creation has been groaning together in the pains of childbirth until now. And not only the creation, but we ourselves, who have the first fruits of the Spirit, groan inwardly as we wait eagerly for adoption as sons, the redemption of our bodies." We will face troubles. In today's society, with a dependence on wealth in an unreliable economy, financial troubles affect even the most wealthy. Yet praise God that wealth is not what we need to be saved. Being free of financial worries is not a requirement to get into heaven. In fact, Jesus more often speaks of the difficulties of having wealth to the point of telling us in Matthew 19:24: "Again I tell you, it is easier for a camel to go through the eye of a needle than for someone who is rich to enter the kingdom of God." We may never get out of a tough financial situation in this life, or perhaps we may receive a phone call that a mysterious benefactor has agreed to pay off all our debt. But our biggest and most troublesome debt, the debt that will matter for all eternity, has already been paid. The benefactor is not mysterious. His name is Jesus. He lived through any trouble you or I could ever experience and more, to the point of suffering and giving His very life. He did this to save us, not from the banks or the bill collectors but from death. Death is a far more permanent trouble than any this earth could offer.

Mother Teresa, in living a life of servitude among some of the poorest people on earth, is commonly attributed with saying this about our eternal condition if we receive the salvation Jesus freely offers: "In light of heaven, the worst suffering on earth, a life full of the most atrocious tortures on earth, will be seen to be no more serious than a single night in an inconvenient hotel."

And for those of us that feel we will never be set free from the burdens of this earth and our debt, rest in the comfort that Jesus offers:

> In my Father's house are many rooms. If it were not so, would I have told you that I go to prepare a place for you? And if I go and prepare a place for you, I will come again and will take you to myself, that where I am you may be also. (John 14:2-3)

Engage

Discussion

Before meeting with your group or partner, review the following questions. Write down your answers as well. When you meet, be ready to share your answers and listen to others.

1. How has society shaped your focus on finances? How has your church?
2. Do you think the modern church has done a good job at showing people how to handle finances?
3. Why do you think movements such as the prosperity gospel are so successful?
4. In what ways can the life of Jesus shift how we view the importance of personal finance?
5. What is the biggest single thing, right now, that you can change to make your finances more God-centered?

Reflection

So much of current nonfiction, even within Christianity, is devoted to the topic of finances. It is obviously important to people. With that said, this chapter adds to the conversation by offering some practical ways in which twenty-somethings can start their individual financial journeys from an easier starting point.

As we embark, write a list of the things you spend money on in a given week. Add up the amount spent on things considered "nonessential." Multiply that out over a year and talk among the group about the things God could use that amount for in your ministry. Talk about how your life would change if you based your financial decisions on God's plan for you.

Activity

For one week, pray before every single financial decision you make, from paying bills to buying coffee. Pray that God would guide you towards whether or not you should actually spend that money. Write down the things God guides you not to purchase and pray about where He would have you put the extra money.

Before You Read Chapter Five

Are you doing the work you thought you would be doing while you were in college? Is the work you do as rewarding as you thought it would be when you started? Are you currently trying to find some work and at a loss over what you should sacrifice in picking a job? Do you really have to sacrifice anything?

God wants us to be happy … and not just on Fridays. He wants us to be as joyful waking up at 6:45 on Monday morning as we are driving home at 5:30 on Friday afternoon. Why is it that work is something we dread so much? We spend so much time doing it, shouldn't we use the time to glorify Him as much as possible?

As you read this chapter, put yourself into a situation where you are doing exactly the work you want to be doing. Would your happiness grow? Would your worship of God be enhanced? How much of your identity is in your current job or in the one you desire?

CHAPTER 5

AS PRETTY AS AN AIRPORT—CAREER AND THE QLC

"Prepare your work outside; get everything ready for yourself in the field, and after that build your house."
Proverbs 24:27

Introspection

Kindergarten is when children are typically confronted with that age-old question: "What do you want to be when you grow up?" Rarely is the answer the same as the career that kindergartener inevitably ends up in. If what we predicted as kindergarteners actually came true, our world would have far too many astronauts and far too few dental hygienists. As a kindergartener, I remember fondly saying with great confidence what I would be when I grew up: a ninja.

As you can probably deduce, that dream didn't quite come true. *At least not yet.*

As an adult of almost thirty years of age, I can look back fondly on a string of jobs that changed often, changed quickly, and have left me with few of what I would call "important skills." Sure, I could deliver you a pizza, bag your groceries, sell you an antique beer stein, wrap your Christmas presents, lay mulch in your lawn, sell you a set of awesome knives, build you a web page, shine your shoes, mix you an appletini, help you with your golf swing, serve you a steak dinner, create a triple-large half-caffe mocha latte, or schedule your chiropractic appointment. But none of these jobs ever had me feeling like I was doing something of value. They may be skills, and to some people they may seem important. I just remember having a lot of trouble kicking the thought that the time I spent doing these things was being wasted.

For many in today's society, these feelings are becoming more and more common. You finish college with aspirations of changing the world, and six months later find yourself in nearly the same job you had when you left for college in the first place. Many colleges today now offer in excess of *one hundred* different majors. Not only does this provide a graduating senior with far more career options than our parents ever dreamt of, it ultimately means that as soon as their degree is in their hand, exiting seniors are faced with one of the most difficult questions they will ever have to answer:

"What do you want to be when you grow up?"

In our "New Economy," with its intense globalization and inherent instability, having a career last your entire lifetime is becoming more and more of a pipe dream. Add to that the lingering societal pressures that one should be successful by the time he or she is thirty, and you can begin to see the overwhelming prospects that the idea of a career can hold. This feeling of being overwhelmed rings true for those who take the first job offered to them out of college, an oftentimes knee-jerk decision which can very easily devolve into years of ever-changing, dead-end jobs.

The development of career worries in a QLC can come from several factors. One factor is that you have had roughly the past seventeen years of your life to learn how to navigate the education system, and then you are suddenly thrown into the work world with little understanding of how to succeed. It's like training your entire life to be an Olympic skier, and then being expected to win the gold medal in hockey. Another reason this transition can be difficult is because when you finish school, the career you spent four years studying to get into is not the only job you are offered, if it is even available. I spent four years studying for a degree in psychology, and it got me a job at a coffee shop. My degree had, at the time, been turned into expensive refrigerator art. You may even have become accustomed to living the life of a college student – sleeping until noon, having your schedule determined by your professors, procrastinating until the last moment with your already-lenient deadlines. And then, you enter a workforce where you are not only called to meet mandatory deadlines but to create your own schedules, social and otherwise.

Christians are faced with a unique factor which can contribute to those feelings of anxiety and confusion with regard to a career. We wonder if this is what God wants us to be doing. "I'm serving people hot beverages," you tell yourself. "I am supposed to be living a life of servitude, acting out the Great Commission! How can I do that when I spend eight hours a day smelling like a coffee bean?"

And there, in that very question, we can begin to see how we are making a difference. Your trouble isn't with what you do, or where or with whom you work. Your trouble is on the inside, with how you feel about your job. You tell yourself that your job isn't important, neglecting to remember that we, and the jobs that we do, are all important in the body of Christ. As Paul tells us in 1 Corinthians 12:18: "But as it is, God arranged the members in the body, each one of them, as he chose." We are put in the life that we have been put into, with the set of circumstances that we have been uniquely given, and are told to honor God with all we have. You may tell yourself that what you are doing matters less than those who are pastors or missionaries or firefighters or police officers. But, in this statement, you forget that your reward for the work you do in God's name, even the work you do here – no matter how insignificant it may seem – comes from God. Colossians 3:23-24 tells us: "Whatever your task, put yourselves into it, as done for the Lord and not for your masters, since you know that from the Lord you will receive the inheritance as your reward; you serve the Lord Christ."

Perhaps your struggle is not in keeping your job, or even in being happy doing it. Perhaps your struggle comes from finding it difficult to know how to serve God with the job you are now doing. Through a set of circumstances which can only be attributed to God, I went from working at a coffee shop to teaching kindergarten in one of my city's most unique and beautiful communities. The student and faculty population represents one of the most diverse groups of people I have ever had the chance to know and love. It is beautiful in that it is right in the heart of the city, overlooking one of its most breathtaking parks. However, even in that place, I would find myself struggling with the idea that I was spinning my wheels with regards to discipleship. It is a diverse school, which means it is also a politically and religiously pluralistic school. I have to be careful about what I say in regard to faith.

After a lot of prayer and introspection, God told me how wrong I had been. We sometimes feel, as Christians, that we are called to be on-the-job missionaries. Whether we are bartenders, cubicle-dwellers, teachers, professional musicians, or janitors, we must juggle our duties of work and our duties as representatives of God.

I, for one, couldn't keep up with the juggling.

I came to realize that I am called during this season of my life to be a school teacher. I am now walking into a new calling as an author and praying about into entering full-time ministry. I can already see my future resume resembling my college in its variety. Old habits die hard. However, part of doing whatever job God calls you into for His Kingdom is realizing that His will for your life may not look like what you think it should look like, but it will always be the best possible path for you. Someone may see the variety in my resume as a sign of me being bored in my work. But I see it, as you should, too, as being open to the guidance and direction God gives you. For me, the journey has had a few more stops along the way than it may have for you. But if seeking God's will is a priority, we share the same destination and approach it with the same humility and hope.

You must also remember what you have *not* been called to do. If God wanted you to be a preacher, He would have called you to go to seminary. If God wanted you to be a businessperson, you would have been guided to seek out business school. He will not simply guide you into the job, He will guide you into the things you will need to do that job as best you can. Finally, if you sincerely seek His guidance, you will find that God calls us into many different jobs. Some of us are *called* to work in coffee shops. Some of us are *called* to be electricians. You are personally responsible to have the kind of relationship with God that enables you to find out from Him exactly how, when, where, and to whom He wants you to minister.

God shows us *how* to minister in Matthew 5:16: "In the same way, let your light shine before others, so that they may see your good works and give glory to your Father in heaven." He shows us *when* to minister in 1 Peter 3:15: "But in your hearts sanctify Christ as Lord. Always be ready to make your defense to anyone who demands from you an account of the hope that is in you." He shows us *where* to minister through such stories as Paul and Silas evangelizing in prison (Acts 16). Basically, we are to be witnesses to His glory everywhere we go. Finally, God shows us *to whom* we are to minister in Matthew 28:19: "Go therefore and make disciples of all nations, baptizing them in the name of the Father and of the Son and of the Holy Spirit."

As you can see, although you do not have to worry about presenting sermons to your coworkers every day, living a life that is a witness to God is a lifelong, moment-by-moment process. You will fall, and in those moments you can be reminded of how amazing God's grace is. However, you should never forget that no matter what your vocation may be, your Boss is the Lord, and your paycheck is in heaven.

It is difficult to predict in our modern culture of instant gratification and economic instability whether any of us will hold a career for our whole lives. It is more difficult to predict, and likely impossible, whether the time spent in a career will always be what the world defines as positive and uplifting. Careers can be trying on your walk with God. You will spend more time doing your job than you will with your own family. You may, in this moment, feel at the end of your rope, lost and without purpose in a world which promises success will bring happiness. How can you be confident that staying in your current occupation is what God wants for you? How are you to know when to cash in your chips and seek a career change or when to just tough it out?

In a word: *Wait.*

No book can tell you how to know whether God wants you to change jobs. If you find a book that proposes to tell you that, I feel badly for you if you paid money for it. Only God, in your heart and through your spirit, can determine where your career path should take you. Yet the advice I can give you is the same advice used by kings, leaders, prophets, and most importantly, by Jesus Himself in seeking God's guidance:

> Be still before the Lord, and wait patiently for him; do not fret over those who prosper in their way, over those who carry out evil devices. Refrain from anger, and forsake wrath. Do not fret—it leads only to evil. For the wicked shall be cut off, but those who wait for the Lord shall inherit the land. (Psalm 37:7-9)

Interview

In the process of writing this book, I started to realize that the lives of many people within my generation of the church are inspiring. For a long time it seemed as if cultural relativity and materialism were so inherent in the society around me that it was difficult to find true radicals for Jesus. Yet, through researching the various issues faced by quarter-lifers as well as attempting to access and articulate a Christian response to these issues, I found this generation could very well be the most radical ever.

As a church, Scum of the Earth in Denver, Colorado has a unique name and an even more unique purpose. In its description at http://www.scumoftheearth.net, they exist "to connect with people who have no interest in 'church' by society's definition." Yet, their name also describes one of their main viewpoints as a body of believers, that "being people of faith does not mean we are better than anyone else."

Leanor Ortega Till is one of the pastors at Scum of the Earth. She oversees the church's art ministries and is also involved in women's ministry. As a founding member of a church that strives to facilitate creativity and the utilization of all of its members' spiritual gifts, Leanor has much wisdom to impart about how Christians can represent the Father both in how they serve Him with their spiritual gifts and how they serve Him in their careers.

I started the interview by asking Leanor, a pastor for a church focused on outreach to people who may have been scarred by society and its often negative and selfish tendencies, how she thought a believer's definition of a successful career would differ from a nonbeliever's definition.

> *In my experience, believers define a successful career based on the following criteria:*

1. *Does the career give glory to God?*
2. *Does the career benefit the world or others in some way?*
3. *Does the career use the employee's gifts or talents?*
4. *Does the career allow the employee enough time to care well for loved ones?*
5. *Does the career allow the employee time to spend with God?*
6. *Does the career put the employee in the lives of those who he/she is ministering to?*

There seems to be an obvious paradigm at work when one looks at the believer's foci compared with the nonbeliever. But how much of that has to do with what society tells us success really is? Why did Leanor think society makes wealth and success synonymous?

> *Our American culture confuses wealth with success because to us, success means being able to choose whatever we want. The wealthy are able to choose where they live, how they live, what type of vacation they take, what car they drive, and what they eat. They get to choose what doctor they see, what education their children receive, and to some extent, what job they hold. Those who do not have wealth do not have as many choices, which suggests a less "free" life overall.*

It could be easily shown that quarter-lifers, believers or not, are bound to encounter career stresses. What would Leanor say to someone asking how to survive these stresses?

> *I believe that this world is fallen and that because of this fall "work" will always be hard. We have eight inches of freedom, found in our brain. In order to survive career stress it helps to first understand that work will never, in this lifetime, be easy or without stress. When an employee understands that, he or she can then be open to learning ways to deal with the stress such as prayer, making friends in the worksite, eating well, et cetera.*

I asked Leanor what made her decide to go into ministry and what she would call her job's greatest reward.

> *Because a career in ministry is so much of God's work and so little of ours, I am not sure I ever truly decided to go into ministry. Ministry, namely, the creation of Scum of the Earth Church, fell into my lap. After recognizing this church uses my giftings and challenges me, I became open to raising support so that I might work here as a career. My job's richest reward is leading people in a lifestyle that demands Jesus and glorifies Him.*

Hearing that going into ministry is "so much of God's work and so little of ours" made me think about other vocations. Would a shift in our focus back to God, who gave us all the talents to do whatever job we are currently doing and a reliance on Him to complete the task, help with the difficulties careers can produce? What is one thing believers can do to prepare themselves against our culture's materialistic and career-centered perspective, and how can they hope to remain strong in their faith under these stressors?

> *Don't give in. Don't read the magazines if they cause you to lust or idolize others. Don't watch the TV shows if they cause you to covet or lust. Don't listen to the music if it causes you to grow in anger or rage. Don't shop if it causes you to covet more than you can afford. Be wise. Be smarter than the culture and understand that we internalize what we see and hear.*

Before finishing the interview, I asked Leanor if she had any final advice specific to quarter-lifers. She responded with some very wise words.

> *Give your parents some grace, their wisdom is worth more than you may think.*

Inspiration

In His 33 years on this Earth, Jesus had two jobs: carpenter and rabbi. Anecdotally, we assume Jesus was a carpenter, as the Bible merely offers that Joseph was a carpenter. Justin Martyr, an extra-biblical source, said, "He was in the habit of working as a carpenter when among men, making ploughs and yokes." However the only verse in the Bible which references Jesus' following in the family career line is used as a rebuke against His rabbinical skills:

> On the Sabbath he began to teach in the synagogue, and many who heard him were astounded. They said, "Where did this man get all this? What is this wisdom that has been given to him? What deeds of power are being done by his hands! Is not this the carpenter, the son of Mary and brother of James and Joses and Judas and Simon, and are not his sisters here with us?" And they took offense at him. (Mark 6:2-3)

Jesus' second job, the time He spent as a rabbi, led Him on a three-year career which accomplished more than any of us could claim to accomplish in a lifetime of work. Yet, He did not abandon or trivialize the life He had led as a carpenter, nor did He make light of the careers of those around Him, including fishermen, tax collectors, and soldiers. What, then, can we hope to learn about how best to handle the issue of career from Jesus?

1. Jesus' definition of success shaped His career.

Jesus was not a "success" by today's standards. He was not wealthy, powerful, or famous by the guidelines as we see them in popular culture. The Jews, looking for a political ruler who would come in power to destroy the domination of the Romans, saw Jesus as a failure. Isaiah predicted this when he said: "He was despised and rejected by others; a man of suffering and acquainted with infirmity; and as one from whom others hide their faces he was despised, and we held him of no account." (Isaiah 53:3)

However in His poverty and seeming weakness, He redefined what it is to be successful. Not only did He come to show us the temporality of the things this world would have us believe equate to success, He showed us the different view that those following Him should have. We should not strive for wealth. We should not strive for a higher position. We should strive for a loving servant's heart. It is easy to fall into the trap of thinking we can create our own success. We go to work on Saturdays; we stay late and miss important events in our family's lives.... We pursue what society tells us will make us happy.

We pursue these things so passionately when all along our true success has already been determined. Our real value does not come from without, from promotions or hefty 401K programs. Our real value comes from realizing that God, the same Creator who formed a universe of stars with His hands, knows our name and wants to walk with us.

The Jews sought an earthly ruler. They could not see past their present difficulties to the eternal promise that God can provide. They saw themselves as struggling, struggling in poverty and low social ranking. We see ourselves as struggling, struggling in our jobs with their long hours and small paychecks. We are so nearsighted that we forget how unimportant the things of this world are. Jesus says in Matthew 16:26: "For what will it profit them if they gain the whole world but forfeit their life? Or what will they give in return for their life?" The world would have you believe that if you just tough it out for forty years, plump up that retirement account, forego your family and friends, eventually you will be happy. God tells us that, if we model our lives this way, eventually we will look back and realize it has all come to nothing because we spent far too long ignoring His ever-present blessings in our life.

Jesus defined success as living where God wants us to live. He does not mean geographically, though following God's guidance may sometimes require a change of residence. He means living, day by day, in the assurance that wherever God leads us in our life is exactly where we need to be, and should be where we want to be.

After having given up their jobs to follow Him, Jesus' disciples were speaking with Him one day on a mountain. As many of us would probably ask in the midst of a three-year voluntary unemployment, they were wondering how they were going to make their money, how they were going to survive. Jesus offers this advice:

> Therefore I tell you, do not worry about your life, what you will eat or what you will drink, or about your body, what you will wear. Is not life more than food, and the body more than clothing? Look at the birds of the air; they neither sow nor reap nor gather into barns, and yet your heavenly Father feeds them. Are you not of more value than they? And can any of you by worrying add a single hour to your span of life? (Matthew 6:26)

They come to Him with career troubles, wondering where their paychecks will come from, how they will get food or clothing or a home. And Jesus, in His wisdom, does not respond by saying they should raise money, or that they should moonlight as fishermen, or even that they should put an ounce of their focus into those things. He tells them, succinctly, that they will be successful – happy, fed, and blessed – because God values them.

Jesus' career was defined by this view of success. His message was seldom to the rich, nor was it ever on how to get rich. His message was to the impoverished masses, and He told them how much God loved them.

Troubles may be affecting you right now in your job. You might feel it is in the wrong place, that you deserve more money, or that you are simply unhappy. Remember, even if you spend twenty years doing the backbreaking work of a carpenter, your true success is measured by whether you are where God wants you to be…not where society tells you that you should be.

2. Jesus' cultivation of passion guided His career.

We have all experienced what I like to call Monday mopings. They happen on Sunday night, when you are setting the alarm clock for Monday morning. That feeling of disappointment rushes over you as you experience the dread of the upcoming work week.

For most of us, there will be a point where we will not be happy to get up and go to work in the morning. Maybe you have difficulty with the people who work around you. Maybe the job itself is unappealing. Maybe you began the job excited about going to work, and it has become an eight-hour exercise in monotony.

Or maybe it is your own lack of passion causing all the issues you are having. Jesus worked long hours, much to the chagrin of the Pharisees when His work week leaked onto the Sabbath. Yet even in the most tumultuous parts of His career, when He was followed by huge groups of people every place He went, when the disciples woke Him from sleeping because of sea storms, when He was asked to perform miracles at a wedding He was attending – He never lost His passion.

Where does passion come from? You may think it comes from outside of yourself. Or that it comes from the incentives of promotions or vacations. Or from being excited to make it through the week till Friday.

But passion, that feverish love of doing the work of God, comes from our devotion to God. The Bible says in John 5:17, when the Pharisees rebuke Jesus for healing on the Sabbath: "But Jesus answered them, 'My Father is still working, and I also am working.'" Christians serve a God who stays busy. We serve a God who is constantly working in the lives of His people. We serve a God who doesn't take vacations.

Yet, just as the passion in our work comes *from* God, the focus of our work should be *on* God. Just as there are some who have lost all passion in their careers, there are some who would say they have too much. Or, rather, their families would say that. They work seventy-hour weeks, take no vacations, and abandon all other activities for the pursuit of their career. This is not what I mean by saying we need to cultivate our passion. I mean that, in *all* that we do, whether in a cubicle, on a beach, or at the dinner table, we should live our lives passionately devoted to the things of God. We are always working, whether we are clocked in or not. We are working to advance the Kingdom, to bring to earth the things of God. If we are passionate about the things of God, we will be passionate not just about our careers, but about our families, our hobbies, our every breath. John 10:10b gives us this message: "I came that they may have life, and have it abundantly." It does not say He came for us to have prosperous careers, or to be wealthy … but to have abundant lives.

If you live truly in the passion of God, if you live your every moment in awe of your Creator, desiring to spread His spoils of love to all around you, then you cannot help but look forward to Mondays. You also cannot help but be excited to come home either.

3. Jesus' appreciation of experience enhanced His career.

It is common, especially in a world of "the next big thing," to reject the experiences of the past for the wonder of the present. You pursue new jobs and immediately cut all ties with the previous one when a better one is found. Believe me, I didn't waste a second throwing out my purple pizzeria polo shirt after I got the job as a bartender. But, in the focus on what is coming, on striving to make a better and better life for yourself, are you losing vital wisdom which could be gained from your past jobs?

It could very easily be argued that Jesus accomplished far more as a rabbi than He did as a carpenter. The fact that His three years of ministry fill the Gospels and His upbringing as a carpenter is referenced in one verse attests to this fact. Even so, Jesus never forsook the importance of what He did as a carpenter. He came back to it often, from referencing things related to carpentry in His stories, such as the wide and narrow gates into eternity, to His probable usage of Koine ("market" or "common") Greek in order to speak parables to the masses, a vernacular probably learned through working with Joseph.

You may be far too focused on what is next to be able to enjoy or appreciate what is now. Each moment of Christ's life (prior to His ministry) was put in place as an experience which would add to the wisdom He needed to best live out His mission. In the same way, each moment of your life is put in place by God to prepare you to be the person He wants you to be. If you are only living for what is to come, rather than what is, you may miss a chance to learn a particular lesson, to enjoy a particular moment, to savor a particular task.

The sum of these moments is what God will use to make you into who He wants you to become. You may think the groceries you are bagging are simply a boring part of a boring day which could be better spent looking for your next job. You may think making one more sales call is the last thing you could want to do. However, what if that bag of groceries will help someone see an example of heavenly stewardship? What if that sales call is the only real contact the person on the other end will have with another one of God's children today?

It is truly amazing to find yourself in a job you know you love. It is an awesome thing to look around at your coworkers and enjoy being around them. This may be more the exception than the rule. If and when you get to this point, you can look back and see the moments leading you to this point. You can see a career of experiences which, though not always easy, were chances to enrich yourself before God.

For some of you, that moment of loving your job may never happen. Perhaps that is where you are now, feeling stuck and hopeless. May you be reminded that no matter what, for all of us as Christians, those experiences inevitably make us ready to enter God's kingdom … in that company, everyone is doing what they love and loving what they do.

4. Jesus' expectation of eternity fueled His career.

Though culture would probably have you believe otherwise, in the end we will all be on a level career playing field. No matter what your occupation is now, you will one day be a broken and fallen human being, judged by the almighty God.

This news could be reassuring for the taxi driver and devastating for the CEO. What really matters is the condition of their hearts.

It is in this realization that we can hope to shift our focus. We have talked about the importance of true success, the importance of passion, and the importance of experience. But more than that, we must spend our lives working as though eternity counted on it...because it does.

Planning is a good thing. Being prepared financially for your spouse and family are both important and commanded. In His agony on the cross, Jesus made sure His own mother would be taken care of after His death: "When Jesus saw his mother and the disciple whom he loved standing beside her, he said to his mother, 'Woman, here is your son.' Then he said to the disciple, 'Here is your mother.' And from that hour the disciple took her into his own home" (John 19:26-27). Love is our greatest command, and from that love comes taking care of our families.

However, if you focus so much on temporary things, things of this life, to the point that you forsake the eternal things, you will abandon yourself to neglecting what is truly important. Jesus told us to live as though the kingdom of God could come at any moment. He tells us in Matthew 24:35-36: "But about that day and hour no one knows, neither the angels of heaven, nor the Son, but only the Father." He was a Rabbi, but He was a Friend first. He was a Teacher, but He did not focus on His teaching so much that He missed any chance to show someone God's love. He was a Healer, but He allowed Himself to be denied healing so we can have the promise of eternal life, and so we can spend the time God has given us telling all around – through our careers but most importantly through our lives – that they have that promise, too.

Jesus did not focus on the particulars of His job. He healed on the Sabbath; He denied the Pharisees' teachings; He completed His work as His Father led Him; and He was sure never to miss an opportunity to show eternity to someone.

We can find passion in our Father; we can find success in our Father; we can live life as a set of experiences from our Father ... and in the end, we can look back and see it was all worth it while we spend eternity with our Father.

Engage

Discussion

Before meeting with your group or partner, review the following questions. Write down your answers as well. When you meet, be ready to share your answers and listen to others.

1. How did you picture your career looking while in high school? How does that picture compare to what you are experiencing now?
2. What are some ways we can live lives more like Jesus during the nine-to-five hours?
3. In your current job or job search, how closely do your goals match up with the goals you feel God has for your life in general?
4. Do you see your job as providing an opportunity to minister, or do you see it as a ministry in itself? Is there a difference? Explain.
5. If your salary were to be removed completely, would you still feel happy doing the work you currently do? Conversely, if your salary were one million dollars, would your outlook on the job change? What does that say about how you view your job?

Reflection

For generations, people have prided themselves on and placed their identities in a career. Our job becomes so intertwined with our identity that what we do for a living sometimes supersedes who we are as people. Ultimately believers are called to minister. Above and beyond our vocation is a responsibility to bring God's Kingdom of love wherever we go. Reflect on the following questions with your small group.

1. How much of your current job is spent in conversation with God, being guided by Him in the decisions you make?
2. What about you right now looks different to the people with whom you work? Are you seen more as a minister or as a coworker?
3. How would you change your work if God were your boss?

Activity
If you don't already, take your Bible with you to work. Start each day for a week by meditating over Colossians 3:22-24. Write down five specific ways that you can better show God in your workplace.

Before You Read Chapter Six

Throughout this book, we have looked at the trials in our lives and ways in which we can move towards a place of celebrating them rather than being overcome by them.

But what would it look like if we approached all of life in this way? What would it look like to see every single struggle we face for what God can teach us through it? Can we really count on God to give us joy in *every*thing?

As you read this chapter, think back over the chapter in this book you struggle with the most. If God can conquer that in your life, He can conquer anything. If God can conquer anything, then why spend time worrying about whether or not we will make it through?

CHAPTER 6

LIFE AND EVERYTHING LIKE IT—LIFE AND THE QLC

"Do not conform any longer to the pattern of this world, but be transformed by the renewing of your mind. Then you will be able to test and approve what God's will is – his good, pleasing and perfect will."
Romans 12:2

Introspection

So we come to the end, the final chapter. Hopefully, you have found some insight into issues you or someone you know in their QLC are facing. Maybe the issue you are dealing with was not even addressed. Each person is unique, and thus each set of difficulties you face in your life is unique as well. But beyond the differences, beyond the specific issues which may be troubling you, is there something that unifies us? Is there some topic we can all relate to, no matter our phase in life or the crisis we may or may not be in right now?

Francis Schaeffer in *How Should We Then Live? The Rise and Decline of Western Thought and Culture* quoting Edward Gibbon's in his *Decline and Fall of the Roman Empire* (published in 1776-1788) said that the following five attributes marked Rome at its end:

1. A mounting love of show and luxury (that is, affluence);
2. A widening gap between the very rich and the very poor (this could be among countries in the family of nations as well as in a single nation);
3. An obsession with sex;
4. Freakishness in the arts, masquerading as originality, and enthusiasms pretending to be creativity;
5. An increasing desire to live off the state.[4]

Sound familiar? It seems as if the world around us easily could be blamed as a cause for most of our problems. Yet our society is not some self-servicing machine, running headlong on its own power. It is fueled by the lives of the people within it. If you are to change the issues you are facing, you must first look to the life you are living.

I heard a pastor give an analogy to illustrate how we are affected by one another. He explained that, in our lives, we are connected to the people and ideas around us with conduits – or pipes – which can flow in both directions. The people and ideas we are connected to determine what is flowing through those pipes into us. But they also control what is flowing out of us into every other person or idea in our life. If I have an entire set of pipes devoted to gaining wealth, then my interactions with the people in my life will reflect accumulation. If I have many of my pipes connecting to ideas of tithing and stewardship, this too will be reflected in the people in my life. On the other hand, if I connect myself with people whose main focus in life is wealth and success, then all other aspects of my life will have a large focus on these things as well. If I am connected with godly, moral people who help to guide me in the direction that God would have me go, then all parts of my life will exemplify that guidance.

Ultimately, we all have a pipe in our life which runs to God. As the source of our every breath, we are connected to Him whether we acknowledge it or not. And just as the things that come into our own life from all the people and ideas we are connected to determine who we are, they also determine how we interact with God.

What is the meaning of life? It is a question that has been asked for time immemorial, and people have attempted to answer it for just as long. Many answers have been given, from the metaphysical to the absurd. Joseph Conrad author of *Lord Jim* said "A man that is born falls into a dream like a man who falls into the sea."[5] Douglas Adams who wrote *The Hitchhiker's Guide to the Galaxy,* said simply, "42."[6] But, for the Christian, what is the meaning of life?

Is it business success, wealth, good relationships, sex, entertainment, doing good to others? How can purpose, fulfillment, and satisfaction in life be found? How can something of lasting significance be achieved? Even Solomon, the wealthiest, wisest man to ever live, found our worldly pursuits to be ultimately a waste. He said in Ecclesiastes 1:2: "'Meaningless! Meaningless!' says the Teacher. 'Utterly meaningless!'" But yet, he also recognized God has put something into us, a desire and knowledge that this life here on earth is not all that is available to us. Ecclesiastes 3:11 says:

"He has made everything suitable for its time; moreover, he has put a sense of past and future into their minds, yet they cannot find out what God has done from the beginning to the end."

If life has an ultimate purpose, if our drives, passions, and desires have something to be directed towards, then any crisis, any major life change, any stress or difficulty can be approached with that purpose in mind and dealt with accordingly. It doesn't matter if you are having intense depression during a career change or mild disappointment that the fast-food restaurant put mayo on your burger – your purpose in life shapes your reaction to life's events.

You were created to not have stress. When God made you, He did not also create depression, or anxiety, or disappointment. Having a QLC is not natural. What is natural is to commune with a God so holy, loving, and good that you can "freely eat of every tree of the garden" (Genesis 2:16b), meaning you can live a life free of worries – worries about finance, career, even death. But we didn't want that. We, as humans both blessed and tasked with the responsibility of free will, decided that knowledge was a greater desire than simply communing with God. We violated God's trust and were thus separated from His presence. Out of this broken trust came sin, and out of sin came stress, worry, depression, and every difficulty we will ever face in our lives.

If you are having a QLC, it is because we have been separated from God. But, as many of you know well, that is not the end of the story.

Jesus. God's Son. Our Savior. The Sacrificial Lamb. He came to give us purpose. He came to show us what our lives *could* be. He came to show us what our lives *should* be. He came to show us that we could have life as it once was. Revelation 21:7 tells us: "Those who conquer will inherit these things, and I will be their God and they will be my children." Through Jesus, we can be conquerors. Through Jesus, we can reclaim our status as the sons and daughters of the King of Kings.

You may already know just how much God loves you. You may know what your true purpose in life is. But knowing it and living it out are two entirely different things. Quarter-life crises are temporary. Even without any outside help, the average people simply endure it for a few years and are back to some sense of normalcy by the time they are in their mid-thirties. But what next? What about the mid-life crisis? If you aren't applying your true purpose so that it infiltrates, dictates, and circulates through every part of your life, you are destined to struggle.

Each of us has a choice. Life can be pictured as a grand symphony performance in which each of us has a seat to watch God at work in our world. Do we dedicate our lives to Him, sacrifice everything we have so we can get the best seats in the house and watch God's work from the front row? Or do we keep our focus on worldly things, invest more into solving our own problems, creating our own wealth, holding onto what we feel is important, and watch God work from the nosebleed seats?

I know this: that God has enough room on the front row for anyone willing to make the sacrifices to sit there. And, once there, once the sacrifice has been made, we are in for the greatest reward we could possibly imagine. "Then Jesus told his disciples, 'If any want to become my followers, let them deny themselves and take up their cross and follow me. For those who want to save their life will lose it, and those who lose their life for my sake will find it.'" (Matthew 16:24-25)

The desires of our heart will be met; God promises us that. If we desire to solve our own problems, God in His love will surely leave us to our own devices to try it. But He will also weep with us when we realize that we cannot do it on our own. If we desire wealth and think that financial security will solve our problems, God in His love may grant us that wealth. But again, He will weep with us when we realize we still have troubles.

If we desire the life that God has for us, and walk in the way He is guiding us to walk, God in His love will grant us this as well. And He will rejoice with us when we start to see solutions to our problems, and when the things of this world that once seemed monumentally important are "no more serious than one night in an inconvenient hotel" compared to the blissful eternity offered to believers.

Life does have an ultimate purpose. God desires for His children to bring heaven to earth. We are promised an eternal home, to be sure. But we are tasked with letting God's love so shine through us that the physical, sin-scarred earth begins to look like it did in the Garden of Eden. God's love in our lives has such power that the world around us, those hopelessly lost to the pressures of society, can change because of it.

As I said before, all of us have a sort of pipe leading directly to God. That pipe is meant to deliver our devotion and worship to God and bring the purity of His love and mercy into our lives. In turn, His love can then travel to all the people we are connected to and shape all the events in our life. But, sin prevents this perfect transfer. God's love and mercy remain pure until they enter us, where our struggles and doubts and failings pollute it until it is unrecognizable at times. Our devotion and worship become tainted as well, even to the point where our good works are corrupt. In Isaiah 64:6a the prophet says: "We have all become like one who is unclean, and all our righteous deeds are like a filthy cloth." Our difficulties become overwhelming, our doubts lead us astray. We see a society that pours ideas of material success into us and it shapes our lives.

Jesus came to change the paradigm. He puts Himself right into our lives, and cleans out every trace of sin. He makes us pure again, He gives us back the life that God originally intended for us to have.

Probably not every one of your questions have been answered. This book is meant to merely start a conversation towards a Christ-centered approach to the issue of quarter-life crises. The greatest testament to how to survive a crisis of any type comes from those who have actually survived it themselves. And thankfully, we have not only a God who knows the successes of our future, we have a God who has lived through the struggles of our present.

I would like to leave this section with a prayer from a personal hero of mine, Dr. Ravi Zacharias. It is a prayer for the times when we feel so deep in struggle, so entrenched with the worries of this world that we wonder where God is, and why He has left us seemingly alone.

> Your ways mystify me oh Lord
> yes, in some journeys I feel you all the way, never doubted.
> But sometimes You seem to vanish after half way of that journey.
> At other times You appear to me at that very last moment.
> And You know Lord, sometimes I actually fear that You'll let me go over the edge.
> You are very unique My child and I will help you learn from Me with that very uniqueness in mind.
> You see if I took everyone all the way, where is the room for their faith?
> If I took everyone more than half the way, where is the room for their love?
> If I did not let You at times even feel abandoned, where is the room for My Cross?
> You are not what you will someday be.
> I AM who I AM!
> And I know how to get you from who you are to who I AM.
> If you do not understand this, where is your hope?[7]

Interview

Musicians throughout history have held a unique place in society for being able to transcend the typical limits of language in order to convey truths about life. There is something stirring about listening to a good songwriter or poet describe something we ourselves have lived through in a way that we may have never thought, but with which we can completely connect. And, sometimes, a musician is talented enough to become famous for that ability.

Corey Crowder had all the ingredients of success: over 5,000,000 plays of his songs online, international recognition of his music as it was played on TV shows like MTV's *The Real World*, a sponsorship by Takamine guitars … and a wife he had loved since high school.

Why, then, did he feel lost?

"It's weird to look back over seven years and think, 'Wow … I didn't have a "why" or a "what".'"

All the pieces were in place for him to be happy, but the driving force was not God. And so, he found himself searching.

"I was just kind of aimlessly throwing songs out and hoping that they stick."

It was in this land of wandering that Corey recognized the void in his life, the emptiness that looms over all of us at some time. That void may not be as noticeable for some, as it can easily be covered up by what the world tells us is important. But in these times, times of crisis and struggle, those temporary coverings are ripped away, and a gaping depth stares back at us, showing us what is truly missing. He was living his life with no "why," no true purpose. As Solomon says so accurately in Ecclesiastes, he was "chasing the wind."

But it was also in this place that God called him back. It was in this place that Corey realized a truth about our Father. He never stops loving us, even when we stop loving Him.

I wanted to talk with Corey not just because he had such a way with words, or because he had come through this journey and gained some valuable truths, but because he was able to remain genuine in a world of fakes. He was able to stay true to his music and his family while seeking to remain true to his walk with God. His faith wavered, his struggles were difficult, but in the end he emerged an even stronger person than he had ever been before.

Having been a fan of his music for a while, and following his awesome story of God's redemptive power, I wanted to talk with him about the ultimates in life: ultimate purposes, ultimate challenges, ultimate goals. I first asked him how he would define the life purpose of a believer, seeking out the kingdom of God.

> *I think every believer is called to be an ambassador for Christ. We are called to a life of sacrifice. Offering our lives back to God.*

Corey is very open about his redemption, going so far as to post an incredible online video of his testimony. When I saw similarities between his struggles and those of someone in a quarter-life crisis, I wondered how he felt believers are better prepared than seekers to navigate that difficult time of life.

> *As believers we are more prepared for any crisis that may come our way because we are no longer depending on our own strength to work through the crisis. We can rely on the infinite strength of God and look to the Word to provide guidance in our times of distress.*

What would he say to someone seeking out how to best survive their own quarter-life crisis?

> *I would tell them to stay in God's Word and constantly seek the will of the Father. Another practical way to deal with such a crisis would be to stay 'others-focused.' I find that this simple principle has helped me to stay close to God and stay out of self-inflicted troubles.*

It is rare to find someone so passionate about their calling, and it is a sign that someone is happy when they can say they are paid to do what they love most. I wondered what made Corey decide to go into music and what was his job's richest reward.

> *Music became a passion of mine shortly after high school. I found that I was able to express myself and make sense of life through music. My job's richest reward has been to see other's lives affected*

by my music. I am blessed to be a part of the soundtrack to people's lives.

Because Corey is so connected with the world of people our age and has such a rich tapestry of music by which to enrich people's perspectives, I wondered what he thinks is the biggest challenge facing people in their twenties and thirties.

The biggest challenge to people our age today is what I call "pace of life." We are such a fast-paced society. We have access to anything we want and fast! This can be a great thing but it is constantly causing problems. We have neglected our families, our friendships, and our relationship with God due to this age of technology. One of my daily prayers to God is that I will SLOW DOWN. I find that when I slow down I am able to recognize God all around me and stay close to Him.

Inspiration

In examining Christ's methods for approaching and discussing the various issues we have undertaken in this book, we have found many times He has taught us what *to* do by showing us what *not* to do. Most times, the behaviors needed to accomplish the goal of eliminating these stresses, and thus triumphing over our QLC, have been behaviors epitomized in Christ's own life. Yet, the even simpler answer to any question that may be raised on how to face life's troubles can be found in a much louder voice throughout Christ's ministry. We are told to live, to live in Christ and to live as Christ lived. Even though there may not have been specific answers to the myriad problems life can throw at us, there is an answer that can strengthen us to prosper under any circumstance. Just live.

1. Jesus gives us the hope to live.
A life without God offers little meaning. No matter whether one is successful or struggling, if God is not at the center it will all crumble into meaninglessness. Conversely, a life *with* God can offer us meaning and hope whether we are successful or struggling. Christ came so that there might be hope for those who felt hopeless. The Jewish people were seeking salvation from the oppression of the Jewish law and the Roman govern-

ment. They were impoverished, servants of a system of guidelines no one could hope to fulfill. Modern people are seeking salvation from the oppression of a materialistic society and an ideological government. We are in debt, narcissistic, servants to a cultural standard of beauty and fame no one can hope to fulfill. We feel unaccepted, hopeless before the people around us, who are also so self-consumed that they fail to acknowledge the worth we can have through Jesus.

Jesus came to give us hope, meaning and guidance in a world that seems so lacking in it. When asked by Thomas how we can know the way to follow Jesus, He responded quite simply, "I am the way, and the truth, and the life. No one comes to the Father except through me" (John 14:6). He is our Way. He is the only path we need follow in our lives and the only direction worth going in. He is our Truth. He is the mirror to which we can hold up any and all standards society sees as important and judge their true merit. He is our Life. He is all we ever need for success, happiness, and joy, and He is the foundation on which all our other life choices should be made on.

The Bible tells us plainly that the Law under which we judge ourselves through our works (be it governmental, religious, societal or otherwise) can do nothing short of leaving us spiritually dead. The grace under which we can realize our true hopelessness, as well as our true value, can do nothing short of renewing our lives. Paul tells us that what Christ did for us on the cross and in His resurrection, in essence, resurrected us. Romans 7:6 tells us: "But now we are discharged from the law, dead to that which held us captive, so that we are slaves not under the old written code but in the new life of the Spirit."

Ultimately, our hope in life is that God, through Jesus' sacrifice, has our lives mapped out. Each difficulty and trial is a result of sin's influence in the world, but through each difficulty and trial God can work to further make us into a people suitable to worship in His presence for eternity. Suffering can and will come in this lifetime. But just as sure as our salvation, we can be confident that God is working in us to change us for the better.

Jeremiah 29:11 tells us: "For surely I know the plans I have for you, says the Lord, plans for your welfare and not for harm, to give you a future with hope." That hope had its first glimmer in the manger at Christ's birth. It had its fulfillment in the empty tomb and can be claimed by anyone who desires it...no matter how hopeless life may seem.

2. Jesus gives us the ability to live.

As we said earlier, Christ's was a ministry of action. Words and sermons were used, but the true crux of His purpose was to show us how to live as though God lived in us. His miracles serve as a beautiful portrait of this perfect life.

In His ministry of miracles, Christ never did magic tricks, bending the laws of nature for the sake of provoking a response in people. His miracles showed us the life we can hope for in God. Our lives were not originally designed to have troubles. We were not created to deal with sickness, or sadness, or death. Yet as we know, because of the invasiveness of sin in the world, those things exist and not one of us remains unaffected by them.

Christ showed us that life can be better, that life *should* be better, and He gave us the ability to make it better. He showed us that we can have a life free of hunger by feeding a multitude with a few loaves and fishes (Matthew 14:13, Mark 6:30, Luke 9:10, John 6:1). He emphasized that the life God has planned for us contains no sickness (Matthew 8:16), blindness (Luke 18:35), deafness (Mark 7:31), or death (Luke 8:40, 49).

Christ's miracles were never intended to be seen as an exception to the natural order of things. They were to be seen as a return to the original order of things. Though we may not be able to escape the impact of these things in our lives here on earth, we have been given the power to overcome them in our expectation of eternity. However, as Christians, we are equipped with the righteousness and strength of Christ in our lives and are given the ability to live the life that God intends for us to live. We can and will overcome the troubles which remain in this world because of the fact that we have had the ways of God imparted into our spirit. First John 4:17 gives us a picture of the power and responsibility Christ has offered to us: "Love has been perfected among us in this: that we may have boldness on the day of judgment, because as he is, so are we in this world."

Our ability to live rests in Christ's willingness to die. Because He came into humanity, with all its limits and restrictions, He was able not only to live and experience life as we do, He was able to die and experience death as one day we undoubtedly will. Yet, it is in this very death that we have been given the true purpose and ability to live. John 12:31-32 gives us a glimpse of the power Christ has for us if we simply accept it: "Now is the judgment of this world; now the ruler of this world will be driven out. And I, when I am lifted up from the earth, will draw all people to myself."

3. Jesus gives us the strength to live.

We have been given hope, and we have been given the ability to live. But what about when we feel weak? What about the times when life feels so oppressive it seems much easier to just give up?

We must first remember that the hope and ability to live do not come from our own selves. Sometimes weakness arises when a situation seems too difficult for *us* to handle. We can never forget that it is not our strength that makes us holy; it is not our effort that brings righteousness. We must work and we must act, but we also must realize the only reason we are able to work and act is because the Spirit of God has given us life and filled us with strength. Just as it was only by God's power Christ was raised from the dead, it is only by God's power we can hope to have the life God wants us to have. In our sinful and mortal frames, we have no strength to survive on our own. However, Romans 8:11 tells us: "If the Spirit of him who raised Jesus from the dead dwells in you, he who raised Christ Jesus from the dead will also give life to your mortal bodies through his Spirit who dwells in you." Once we truly realize our strength comes from the Source of all strength, and our power from the Source of all power, the struggles of our life can become easier to navigate.

Jesus faced the struggle of death. He not only faced death, He faced one of the most gruesome and torturous forms of death imaginable. It is in looking at how He handled this, how He found the strength to endure, that we can learn how to endure our own difficulties. First, He was able to face His suffering because He knew it was His purpose. He knew the struggles were a part of a grander plan. He says in John 12:27-28: "Now my soul is troubled. And what should I say— 'Father, save me from this hour'? No, it is for this reason that I have come to this hour." Second, He was able to face His suffering because He knew it was temporary. John 14:18-19 shows us Jesus speaking about His resurrection: "'I will not leave you orphaned; I am coming to you. In a little while the world will no longer see me, but you will see me; because I live, you also will live." Thirdly, Jesus was able to face His suffering because He knew what the end result would be. As He spoke with a lonely Samaritan woman who was drawing water from a well, Jesus tells her of the life He provides for us all: "Everyone who drinks of this water will be thirsty again, but those who drink of the water that I will give them will never be thirsty. The water that I will give will become in them a spring of water gushing up to eternal life" (John 4:13-14). Finally, Jesus was able to face His suffering because He was strengthened by the love of God. He showed us how to love so we could have the prime example of how to love one another. It is important to remember that love is not only our duty, it is our greatest commandment. Jesus told His disciples in Matthew 22:37: "You shall love the Lord your God with all your heart, and with all your soul, and with all your mind." Its importance in our example for others – and the strength for ourselves – cannot be overstated.

If we want the strength to face the trials of this human life, we must simply follow the example of Christ. We must realize struggle is inevitable and part of a larger purpose, that it is temporary, and that the end result is something better than we could ever hope for. We have the privilege and duty to love all around us as God loves us. Because of these things, Christ was able to walk to the cross. He walked there alone, forsaken by His disciples. Because of that, we can walk in the strength of knowing we can never be forsaken…or alone.

4. Jesus gives us the reason to live.

Our life can be filled with hope, blessed with ability, and enriched by strength. Yet without a true purpose, all those things go to waste. Society would say the reason we are alive is to better ourselves, to contribute to the greater culture, and to make ourselves as happy as possible. Jesus would agree with one of those three things. He does command us to contribute to the greater culture, but in a different way than society would have us believe. He tells us the reason we are alive is to better the world around us by proclaiming the message He has brought. He also tells us our own happiness should by no means be our focus.

This drastic switch of perspective results in a paradigm that cannot help but cultivate our purpose and goals, making them more in line with those God has for us. We are called to a life which strives for perfection. Matthew 5:48 says: "Be perfect, therefore, as your heavenly Father is perfect." Life is given through Christ, but it is accomplished through a denial of the nature sin has left us with. This nature will forever provide opportunities to pursue materialism, narcissism, and all the other "isms" the world promises can make us happy. It is not until we sacrifice the things of earthly importance and die to this nature of sin, that we can have any real reason to live. Paul tells the Philippians, "For to me, living is Christ and dying is gain." (Philippians 1:21)

As Christians, we are called to a life of servitude. As our Sacrifice, Christ lived a life of servitude so we can have an example to follow. We are called to follow the example of Christ in how we interact with God and the world around us. Second Corinthians 5:15 says: "And he died for all, so that those who live might live no longer for themselves, but for him who died and was raised for them." In truly and earnestly dedicating our lives to the cause of loving servitude, we can not only escape the clutches of cultural oppression, we can know what it means to be happy and to start bringing God's Kingdom to a godless world.

Engage

Discussion
Before meeting with your group or partner, review the following questions. Write down your answers as well. When you meet, be ready to share your answers and listen to others.

1. What, right now, is keeping you from really experiencing life?
2. The Scriptures tell us we have been brought from death to life in our salvation. How can knowing that change how we look at crises?
3. What are some ways you can live more fully in each of the areas we have discussed throughout the book?
4. How will you avoid a mid-life crisis?
5. How would you now define this time in your life when others ask?

Reflection
Believers of Jesus are called to a life which looks different from normal – or even successful – by society's definition. But in that anomaly comes a joy unachievable by any earthly pursuits. Living in that place brings with it the responsibility of offering a reason to others for why we carry that hope. Go around in your small group and take about five minutes each for a time of sharing. Give the reasons for your hope as if the person you are talking to has never heard the name of Jesus. Enter into a time of prayer, asking God to give you opportunities to share those words with others.

Activity
Go back through the notes you have taken during this study. Put them in a place where they can be found easily. Within each chapter's notes, write down ways in which you can now celebrate those things rather than suffer

through them. Encourage people within your group with these things. Live life in celebration!

CONCLUSION

24-HOUR JESUS PEOPLE

"You are the light of the world. A city on a hill cannot be hidden. Neither do people light a lamp and put it under a bowl. Instead they put it on its stand, and it gives light to everyone in the house. In the same way, let your light shine before men, that they may see your good deeds and praise your Father in heaven."
Matthew 5:14-16

A lot has been said in this book about society, and much of it may sound quite negative. I don't hold anything but sincere love for the world in which humanity exists. Yet, it is a cautionary, skeptical outlook I hold, due in part to a Christian's responsibility. There are many schools of thought concerning Paul's lesson to "be in the world but not of it." How is it possible in such a globalized and interconnected society to remain set apart as the standards for living that God instructs us to be? Furthermore, how can we ever hope to relate to those around us who have not yet heard the message of God's love if we are so distanced from the things our culture values that we are basically speaking a different language? Wouldn't it be easier for us to survive crises of self-worth if we weren't even exposed to what society claims is valuable?

We are the representatives of God's Kingdom in this world. Jesus tells us in John 17:14-16:

> I have given them your word, and the world has hated them because they do not belong to the world, just as I do not belong to the world. I am not asking you to take them out of the world, but I ask you to protect them from the evil one. They do not belong to the world, just as I do not belong to the world.

We do not belong to this world. It isn't that we are to separate ourselves from the world, or not to enjoy seeing God's creative power in the culture around us. But we must also remember we do not belong to this world. Once brought under the saving grace of Jesus, we become not only new creations, but members of a new family: the family of God. Our permanent residency will be the Kingdom. Just as we are still ourselves when we leave our earthly homes to go to work, school, or elsewhere, we are still God's children when we are not in church. For too long, society has pressured those who profess a set of religious beliefs to keep those beliefs as a separate category like those of education, economic class, and occupation. It is time for Christians to remember that our belief in God is not separate from any other area of our life. It is the framework onto which we should place all other parts of our life. Until we do this, we cannot ever hope to escape struggle. We are not to engage in the sinful activities the world promotes, nor are we to retain the insipid, corrupt mind the world creates. Rather, we are to conform ourselves and our minds to that of Jesus Christ.

It is in this place where I learned the greatest lesson my QLC has taught me. In my attempts at being in the world and not of it, I had forsaken the God who was to be my foundation in each of my life's moments. It was not until I realized it was me, not God, trying to hold all these things together that I began to see a glimmer of hope that the crisis could be survived.

I learned that God is relentless, overwhelming in His love.

Our God is devoted.

Our God embodies love as a noun and fulfills love as a verb.

Our God knows the names of all the stars, and counts the hairs on all our heads.

In His wisdom, our God formed us out of the dirt. In His empathy, He spent a life walking through our dirt. In His grace, He let His sacrificial blood fall to the dirt. Then in His love, He picks us up from that dirt.

God loved me in spite of the fact that I was pulling away. He was the Father waiting on His prodigal son to return from wasting his inheritance on things he thought were valuable. He was the Shepherd who wasn't content to return with only ninety-nine sheep but searched until the one hundredth was returned.

Just as our God is furiously in love with us, we are to live furiously in love with Him, dedicating our every moment to letting His Kingdom break forth in this world. It was in welcoming the enormous power of

God into my life that I realized how insignificant the struggles of my own life seemed in comparison.

It is my earnest hope that, as Christians in a world of disbelief, as humble servants in a world of materialism, as givers in a world that seems to only take, we can always remember that the God of true strength, power, success, and eternity is also our Father.

Just as God has blessed me with the experiences which resulted from my QLC, it is my hope, He will bless you as well. It is said one cannot appreciate the lessons of a trial until reflecting on them in hindsight. I pray you will have that joy and have it soon. I also pray God will use you to further this conversation with others in your life who will come to encounter the unique challenges of the quarter-life crisis. We learn from experience, we teach from experience; and we learn from teaching. I appreciate God granting me the opportunity to write this book simply because I have been able to learn more about myself in the process. I hope you come to learn more about yourself as well.

We live in a world groaning with stress. We live on a planet so entrenched in the power of sin it is moaning for God's return. Each of us feel it, whether in a quarter-life crisis, divorce, mid-life crisis, loss of a loved one, or any multitude of pains. Thanks be to God, that the very Creator of the cosmos, a God who formed a universe of perfect suitability, used those same hands to create His most wonderful masterpiece: you. With the same voice He used to command galaxies into existence, He whispered in a still, small voice into a saddened, angry, frustrated 28-year-old's ear to show him what love is truly supposed to feel like.

He did. I heard it. And so can you.

FOR FURTHER READING

MORTALITY

Richard Beck, *Unclean: Meditations on Purity, Hospitality, and Mortality* (Cascade Books, 2011).

David Crowder and Michael Hogan, *Everybody Wants to Go to Heaven, but Nobody Wants to Die* (Zondervan, 2009).

C.S. Lewis, *A Grief Observed* (HarperOne, 2001).

N.T. Wright, *Surprised By Hope: Rethinking Heaven, the Resurrection, and the Mission of the Church* (HarperOne, 2008).

MARRIAGE

Gary Chapman, *Covenant Marriage: Building Communication & Intimacy* (Broadman and Holman, 2003).

Timothy Keller, *The Meaning of Marriage: Facing the Complexities of Commitment with the Wisdom of God* (Dutton Adult, 2011).

Gary Thomas, *Sacred Marriage: What If God Designed Marriage to Make Us Holy More Than to Make Us Happy* (Zondervan, 2000).

Ravi Zacharias, *I, Isaac, Take Thee, Rebekah: Moving from Romance to Lasting Love* (Thomas Nelson, 2005).

AUTONOMY

Norman L. Geisler, *Chosen But Free: A Balanced View of God's Sovereignty and Free Will* (Bethany House, 2010).

Louie Giglio, *I Am Not But I Know I Am: Welcome to the Story of God* (Multnomah Books, 2005).

Joe Thorn, *Note to Self: The Discipline of Preaching to Yourself (Re.Lit)* (Crossway Books, 2011).

Bruce Wilkinson, *You Were Born for This: Seven Keys to a Life of Predictable Miracles* (Multnomah Books, 2009).

FINANCE

Randy Alcorn, *Money, Possessions, and Eternity* (Tyndale House Publishers, Inc., 2003).

Timothy Keller, *Counterfeit Gods: The Empty Promises of Money, Sex, and Power, and the Only Hope that Matters* (Riverhead Trade, 2011).

Dave Ramsey, *The Total Money Makeover: A Proven Plan for Financial Fitness* (Thomas Nelson, 2009).

John R. Schneider, *The Good of Affluence: Seeking God in a Culture of Wealth* (William B. Eerdmans Publishing Company, 2002).

CAREER

Jon Acuff, *Quitter* (Lampo Press, 2011)

Seth Godin, *Linchpin: Are You Indispensable?* (Portfolio Hardcover, 2010)

Dan Miller, *48 Days To The Work You Love* (B&H Books, 2005).

Gene Edward Veith, Jr. *God at Work: Your Christian Vocation in All of Life* (Crossway Books, 2011).

LIFE

Max Lucado, *Outlive Your Life: You Were Made to Make A Difference* (Thomas Nelson, 2010)

Paul Miller, *A Praying Life: Connecting with God in a Distracting World* (NavPress, 2009).

John Piper and Justin Taylor, *Stand: A Call for the Endurance of the Saints* (Crossway Books, 2008)

Dallas Willard, *The Divine Conspiracy: Rediscovering Our Hidden Life In God* (HarperOne, 1998).

ENDNOTES

1. Elizabeth Kubler-Ross, *On Death and Dying* (NewYork: Scribner, 1997), 6.
2. Robert O. Blood, *Love Match and Arranged Marriages: A Tokyo-Detroit Comparison* (New York: Free Press, 1967), 118.
3. Eric Berne, *Games People Play* (London: Corgi, 1964), 78.
4. Francis Schaeffer, *How Should We Then Live? The Rise and Decline of Western Thought and Culture* (Illinois: Crossway Books, 1983), 201.
5. Joseph Conrad, *Lord Jim* (New York: International Collectors, 1920), 163.
6. Douglas Adams, *The Hitchhiker's Guide to the Galaxy* (New York: Harmony, 2004), 141.
7. A prayer by Ravi Zacharias from his message "Mind the Gap" (CD 165), given at Founders' Weekend (November 8, 2003), Charleston Place Hotel, Charleston, SC.